Text © 2020 Jennifer Copley, Vancouver, British Columbia, Canada

ALL RIGHTS RESERVED. This book contains material protected under International and Federal Copyright Laws and Treaties. Any unauthorized reprint or use of this material is prohibited. No part of this book may be reproduced or transmitted in any form or by any means, electronic or mechanical, including photocopying, recording, or by any information storage and retrieval system without express written permission from the author.

Images are copyright of the photographers cited below each photo. The majority are portraits of our resident cats and the kittens we have fostered for the Vancouver Orphan Kitten Rescue Association (VOKRA). The rest were provided by photographers who have made their images freely available online with various copyright-friendly licenses.

Resident cat Sage, willing to pose in a pirate hat for treats, Jennifer Copley

Table of Contents

Chapter 1: Love and Affection 5
Do cats feel love and other "human" emotions? 6
Are male or female cats more affectionate? 13
How can I encourage my cat to be more affectionate? 13

Chapter 2: Intelligence 15
Are cats intelligent? 16
Which cat breeds are the most intelligent? 19
Which are smarter: cats or dogs? 29

Chapter 3: Anger, Fear, and Anxiety 32
Why do cats hiss? 33
Why do some cats attack when being petted 33
Why do cats fight? 35
How can I prevent cat fights? 38
How can I reduce my cat's separation anxiety? 40
Why do some cats become anxious or phobic? 42
Why are cats afraid of cucumbers? 43

Chapter 4: Communication 45
What is my cat trying to tell me when he meows? 46
What is my cat saying with her body language? 47
Do cats sulk? 51
Why do some cats howl, especially at night? 52

Chapter 5: Social Behaviours 54
Do cats prefer to be alone? 55
How can I encourage my new cat and my resident cat to bond? 58

Why do cats rub against things? 60
Why do cats roll on their backs to greet people? 61

Chapter 6: Strange Attractions 62
Why do some cats suck on fabric, wool, or hair? 63
Why do cats go crazy for catnip, mint, or valerian? 64
Why do some cats like shoes, socks, or feet? 67
Why do cats love boxes? 68
Why do some cats love bleach or chlorine? 69

Chapter 7: Eating and Drinking 70
Why do cats eat grass or houseplants? 71
Why do some cats eat kitty litter? 72
Why do some cats eat soap? 73
Why do some cats eat plastic? 73
How can I stop my cat from eating inappropriate items? 74
Why do some cats drink from the toilet when they have fresh tap water available? 75
Why will a cat suddenly stop eating? 75
Why do some cats suddenly develop voracious appetites? 77
Why do some cats drink so much and pee so often? 80

Chapter 8: Hunting 83
Why do cats play with their prey? 84
Why do cats make chattering sounds when they see birds through a window? 85
Why do cats bring home live prey? 85

Chapter 9: Behaviour Problems   86

Why do some cats pull out their fur?   87

Why do cats have accidents outside the litter box (and how can they be prevented)?   88

Why do cats scratch furniture and carpets (and how can I stop them from doing this)?   90

Can declawing cats cause behaviour problems?   93

Chapter 10: Cats and Kittens   95

Will tom cats kill kittens?   96

Will handling newborn kittens cause their mother to reject them?   98

Why do mother cats move kittens?   99

At what age can cats start having kittens?   100

Chapter 11: Cats and Dogs   101

Can cats and dogs be friends?   102

How should I introduce a new dog to my cat?   103

Which cat breeds get along best with dogs?   104

Which dog breeds get along best with cats?   105

How can I stop my cat from attacking my dog?   108

How can I stop my dog from attacking my cat?   109

Chapter 12: Miscellaneous Cat Quirks   111

Why do cats sometimes appear to be grimacing with their mouths open?   112

Why do cats make sudden mad dashes around the house?   112

Why do cats knead or paddle with their paws?   113

Why does a tom cat bite a female's neck while mating?   114

Why do some cats play with water?   114

Why do cats chew on their claws?   115

Why do cats gravitate to people who fear or dislike them?   116

Why do cats purr?   116

Chapter 13: Other Frequently Asked Questions   120

Do cats like music?   121

Does spaying or neutering affect a cat's behaviour and personality?   122

Can indoor cats be happy?   124

Do cats have psychic intuition?   129

Are there links between fur colour and personality?   131

How many hours do cats sleep?   136

Do cats dream?   137

Do cats always land on their feet?   137

Do cats use their whiskers for balance?   138

Do cat personalities differ by breed?   140

Do cats age 7 years for every human year?   142

About the Author   143

Resident cat Sage snuggles with a foster kitten named Catisse, Jennifer Copley

Chapter 1: Love and Affection

Resident cat Freya washes a foster kitten named Rambler, Jennifer Copley

Do cats feel love and other "human" emotions?

Foster kitten McKonky hugs resident cat Sage, Jennifer Copley

There is evidence that cats experience many of the same emotions that humans do, though probably in simpler forms. Cats show love in various ways, including affectionate body contact, seeking or attempting to provide comfort, bringing presents, and grieving the loss of someone close.

Affectionate body contact

Unlike dogs, most cats don't try to appease their owners, so they can seem indifferent or aloof, but they make a number of affectionate gestures, including head butting, lap sitting, purring, touching noses, and rubbing against people and other cats.

When cats rub against other cats, it's called allorubbing, and it reinforces a group bond and identity by transferring scents. Allorubbing can be likened to a hug or a handshake among humans. When cats do this with people, they're indicating that they view those people as part of their clan.

Bringing presents

Modern domestic cats tend to view their owners as surrogate parents and themselves as permanent kittens that are fed, groomed, and comforted when upset. However, some cats take on the parental role of caring for their owners by bringing "presents," usually dead rodents and birds or live prey animals. In the latter case, the cats may be providing opportunities for hunting practice, as a mother cat would for her kittens.

Providing comfort

There is widespread anecdotal evidence that many cats try to comfort unhappy people by rubbing against them, purring, sitting on their laps, winding around their legs, and engaging in other behaviours targeted specifically to the unhappy individual. Of course, some cats aren't inclined to comfort anyone, but the same can be said of certain people.

Resident cat Laya snuggles with foster kitten Smokey (we adopted Smokey and his sister because Laya liked them), Jennifer Copley

Sage washes a foster kitten named TJ, Jennifer Copley

Love of other animals

Female cats are among the best mothers in the animal kingdom, and some tom cats in feral colonies provide affection and care to their mates and offspring as well. Groups of feral female cats, often blood relatives, usually raise their young collectively. They nest communally, nurse, groom, and guard one another's offspring, and act as midwives for other females when they give birth, cleaning the mother and her newborn kittens. Many cats have also adopted and nursed baby animals of other species, including dogs, mice, squirrels, and pandas.

A foster kitten hugs Freya, Jennifer Copley

Grieving

Cats display signs of grief when they loose loved ones, and if a mother cat's young kittens are taken away from her, she will search frantically and call for them.

Many cats show signs of profound grief after their human companions have died, in some cases becoming severely withdrawn and even refusing food. This indicates that cats are capable of experiencing something more than "cupboard love" for their owners. Many owners have also reported cats grieving after the loss of other household pets.

Of course, not all cats will grieve deeply; some get over things more quickly than others. Like people, individual cats experience grief in different ways and at different intensities.

Young Smokey relaxes with his 21-year-old surrogate mother Laya, Jennifer Copley

Scientific evidence for feline emotions

Evidence suggests that cats can experience many of the same feelings people do, though they can't analyze them or seek meaning from them in the way that humans can because this requires the capacity for abstraction. Cat owners rely primarily on observations of feline behaviour to determine which emotions their cats may be feeling, but there is also physiological evidence indicating that human and feline emotions are similar:

- Biochemical changes that occur in the human brain with certain emotions such as pleasure or fear also occur in cats, and cats produce and respond to the same mood-regulating neurotransmitters (dopamine, serotonin, etc.) as people do.
- Some pharmaceuticals designed to treat psychological problems in humans such as anxiety are also effective for cats.
- Damage to certain brain structures that regulate fear, rage, and other emotions has similar effects on people and cats.
- Cats can experience depression severe enough to override basic survival instincts such as the urge to eat.

The range of feline emotions

Emotions expressed by cats include simple feelings of joy, sadness, anger, fear, anxiety, excitement, affection, frustration, pleasure, and contentment, and many people believe that cats display even more complex social emotions, such as compassion, contempt, embarrassment, jealousy, and love.

Charles Darwin believed that the differences between humans and animals are quantitative but not qualitative. In other words, the experiences of humans and animals fall along different points of a continuum of consciousness, but they are on the same continuum.

There are people who continue to argue that animals don't experience emotions, despite mounting evidence against this view. Many of these individuals have only observed animals in laboratory settings where their behaviour is unnatural due to stress, pain, and lack of social interaction.

Some people cling to the belief that animals don't have feelings to justify inhumane animal experimentation, or because they fear that others will no longer find current hunting and farming practices acceptable if animals have emotional lives. However, many organic farmers have found that well-treated animals in low-stress environments are healthier and more productive.

The Countess Hissyfit displays complicated emotions as she begins to develop trust while still feeling wary, Jennifer Copley

Aurora, a newly arrived feral, shows fear with lowered ears and lack of eye contact, Jennifer Copley

Sage looks annoyed as a pair of playful foster kittens ruin his afternoon nap, Jennifer Copley

Differences between human and animal emotions

The primary difference between the emotions of people and animals is that humans can analyze their feelings and even have emotional responses to their own emotional responses, whereas animals are unlikely to generate this sort of feedback loop. Humans can engage in metacognition because they have a level of self-consciousness that cats don't possess, which enables them to think about the meaning of their emotions as well as their current and future implications.

Seymour looking thoughtful, Jennifer Copley

Many people know that cats experience emotions but misunderstand feline behaviours due to the tendency to anthropomorphize (ascribe human characteristics to animals). Owners may project complex feelings and motivations onto their pets that the animals aren't capable of experiencing or misinterpret an animal's motivations and feelings because they don't understand the differences between animal psychology and human psychology. For example, many owners believe that their cats urinate on the floor out of spite or vengefulness, but this behaviour actually results from anxiety, territoriality, illness, dislike of a particular type of cat litter, or problems with the litter box.

A cat expresses anger impulsively and directly by lashing out, not by plotting revenge, and even aggressive responses usually stem from fear rather than rage. In many cases, the cat is launching a pre-emptive strike against someone she views as a threat rather than acting in anger.

Overall, the evidence indicates that cats can experience many of the same emotions that humans do, including some of the more complex ones such as love. However, it's a mistake to assume that the emotions underlying cat behaviours are always the same as what a person would likely be feeling if he behaved in a similar manner.

A "laughing" foster kitten named Bif the Mighty, Jennifer Copley

References

- Bekoff, M. (2007). *Animals Matter: A Biologist Explains Why We Should Treat Animals with Compassion and Respect*. Boston, MA: Shambhala.
- CatChannel.com. (20 November 2002). "Can Cats Feel Emotion?"
- Crowell-Davis, S., DVM, PhD, DACVB. (1 November 2006). "CVC Highlights: Dispelling the Myth of the Asocial Cat." VeterinaryMedicine.dvm360.com.
- Hartwell, S. (2003). "Do Cats Have Emotions?" MessyBeast.com.
- Horwitz, D.F., DVM, ACVB. (2001). "The Neurological and Pharmacological Basis for Fears and Anxieties." Atlantic Coast Veterinary Conference 2001. VIN.com.
- Rubinowitz, S. (n.d.). "Do Cats Have Feelings?" PetPlace.com.
- Schneck, M., & Caravan, J. (1990). *Cat Facts*. New York, NY: Barnes & Noble Inc.

Proof that cats care: Profiles of feline heroes

Sage gets caught up in a grocery bag while looking for food to steal, turning himself into the world's most ridiculous superhero, Jennifer Copley

Cats often get a bad rap because they're not as obedient or eager to please as their canine counterparts, but many have risked their lives to save people or other animals. Google "Cat saves" and you'll get hundreds of results.

Many cats have stayed in dangerous situations to alert their human families to fires or gas leaks when they could have escaped on their own (in a few cases even sacrificing their own lives to help others). Cats have also assisted their owners during medical crises and fought dogs, snakes, and even humans to save those they love. The following are just a few stories of the many cats that have gained worldwide acclaim for their selfless heroic deeds.

Tara

When 4-year-old Jeremy Triantafilo was attacked by a vicious dog, the family cat Tara came to his rescue. The entire incident was caught on security cameras, which show the boy being dragged from his bike by the dog, the cat body slamming the dog (which caused it to let go of the boy), and the boy's mother running out to him as the cat chases the dog away. Triantafilo required stitches for his bite wounds but made a full recovery (CBC News, 2014).

Lima

Cherry Woods was also viciously attacked by two large dogs and might have been killed had her cat Lima not intervened. Alerted by Cherry's screams, her husband came running out of their home but was unable to drive away the enormous pit bulls. Fortunately, the couple's normally timid cat leapt from the bushes and attacked the dogs, clawing and hissing. The dogs went after Lima, who led them away. Lima returned later, unharmed, and Cherry recovered from her injuries (*People Magazine*, online, 2010).

Tiger

Sophie Thomas, 97, was working in her garden when she was attacked by four large dogs. As Thomas fought for her life, her cat Tiger leapt into the fray, leading the dogs away so that Thomas could escape into the house. As she washed her wounds at the kitchen sink, Tiger returned home, unharmed (AnimalChannel.co, 2017).

Smudge

When 5-year-old Ethan and his 2-year-old brother were set upon by a group of bullies, their cat Smudge raced to the rescue. The boys' mother saw the attack through a window and raced out to help. However, by the time she arrived, the bullies were running away, scratched and sobbing. When others heard about Smudge's heroism, he was nominated for a Cats Protection Charity National Cat of the Year Award (*Daily Mirror*, 2014).

Sosa

A woman (identified only as Kimberley) encountered a poisonous snake in her garden. As the snake was about to strike, her cat Sosa attacked it. Sosa suffered a bite on the paw but recovered after three days in an animal hospital (Petcentric.com, 2009).

Masha

Masha, a cat living in Obninsk, Russia, found an infant abandoned outdoors in the freezing cold. The plump cat covered the child with her body to keep him warm and cried for help, summoning local residents. Masha's intervention ensured that the baby did not freeze to death (*Washington Post*, 2015).

Homer

Gwen Cooper's cat Homer, named after the famous blind Greek author, was a beloved rescue who had lost his eyes to a serious infection. When a man broke into Cooper's home late one night, she woke to find Homer hissing at the intruder. Normally a gentle, mellow cat, Homer launched at the home invader, scratching and biting, which caused him to flee. Homer's life has been immortalized in two books: *Homer's Odyssey: A Fearless Feline Tale, or How I Learned About Love and Life With a Blind Wonder Cat* and *Homer: The Ninth Life of a Blind Wonder Cat*.

Homer's Odyssey by Gwen Cooper

Tom, Tiger, and Fidge

Sue MacKenzie saved Tom's life by taking in the hungry stray during a rainstorm, and more than two decades later, Tom returned the favor. When her 24-year-old cat started obsessively tapping the back of her neck, MacKenzie was sufficiently concerned about his strange behaviour that she took him to a veterinarian. The vet said Tom was fine, so perhaps he was trying to tell her something important. MacKenzie then sought medical attention for herself, receiving a diagnosis of Hodgkins Lymphoma and lifesaving treatment (*Huffington Post,* 2015).

Other cats have also warned their owners of growing cancers, enabling early interventions. Tiger alerted Lionel Adams to a growing cancer by repeatedly scratching a spot over the tumour (CTV News, 2009), and Wendy Humphries was saved when her cat Fidge detected a malignant tumour the size of a pea and began obsessively jumping on her breast until she was concerned enough to get it checked (*Huffington Post*, 2012).

Luna

While the Chappell-Root family slept, a fire broke out in their kitchen. Their cat Luna woke Emily Chappell-Root, who was able to wake the rest of her family so that she and her husband could get their 6 children out to safety before flames consumed their home (*People Magazine*, 2017).

Brat

Brat alerted his human family when their child was having a life-threatening seizure that required immediate medical attention, saving the child's life (*Hero Cats* by Eric Swanson).

Tommy

Tommy dialed 911 to summon help when his owner Gary Rosheisen fell from his wheelchair. Rosheisen had taught Tommy how to call 911 using speed dial but was not sure if the cat would actually be able to do it in an emergency (NBC News, 2006).

Midnight

Midnight howled into a baby monitor, bringing his owners running to find that a mobile above the crib had fallen and tangled around their baby's neck. The child had turned blue and was seconds away from brain damage and death but was rescued in the nick of time due to the cat's cry for help (*Hero Cats* by Eric Swanson).

Salem

Salem rang a cowbell to summon help from the neighbours after his human companion had a nasty fall and lay helpless on the ground (*Hero Cats* by Eric Swanson).

Schnautzie

Greg and Trudy Guy were planning to adopt a puppy but instead fell in love with a little black kitten brought into the pet store by a rescue organization. They fostered Schnautzie and eventually adopted her. Six months later they were woken in the middle of the night by the little cat, who sat on Trudy's chest and tapped her nose until she opened her eyes. Schnautzie then alerted her owners to a growing danger by sniffing frantically. A ruptured gas pipe leading into their house had filled the place with explosive fumes, but the couple was able to escape in time thanks to Schnautzie. Firemen later said that if their water heater or furnace had turned on before they had escaped, there would have been an explosion. Schnautzie's heroism was recognized by the Great Falls Animal Foundation, which gave her a Purple Paw Award at their Annual Fur Ball (*People Magazine*, 2010).

Sally

Craig Jeeves was woken in the middle of the night by his cat Sally, who was jumping on his head and screaming into his face to make sure he understood the seriousness of the situation. Jeeves found his house in flames and just barely escaped with his life. The house was destroyed, and Jeeves was treated for smoke inflammation, but because of Sally's intervention, he made it out alive and he credits Sally with saving his life (*The Guardian*, 2014).

Helper cats

Further evidence that cats care comes from the many felines who voluntarily become helpers for blind or deaf humans or other animals. If you do a YouTube search for "seeing eye cat," you'll find plenty of videos showing cats performing this service, and blindness is not the only disability for which there are helper cats.

Seeing-eye cat Kiki keeps blind companion Whitey from wandering onto the road, geo coop, https://www.youtube.com/watch?v= sCMLUktBsNo

Anecdotal reports from cat owners indicate that many felines become "hearing cats" for deaf owners despite a lack of training. These cats let their owners know when a baby is crying in another room, a doorbell rings, or a fire alarm goes off.

There are also cats that act as therapy animals, visiting hospitals and nursing homes with their owners, and they often zero in on those who need them most. One famous example is Dewey Readmore Books, who was the Official Ambassador for the Spencer Public Library in Iowa and a therapy cat. Dewey not only entertained library patrons and staff with his antics, but also demonstrated a profound sensitivity. Bret Witter and Vicki Myron share a touching anecdote that illustrates Dewey's intuitive compassion: "I will never forget Dewey's friend Crystal, a severely mentally and physically handicapped girl so withdrawn that everyone thought she was dead inside. But Dewey sensed something, and he started following her wheelchair. Then he started climbing up and sitting on her wooden tray. She couldn't control her muscles, so she couldn't pet him, but she would squeal with delight. One day, I placed him inside her jacket. Dewey put his head on her chest and purred, and Crystal...she just exploded. She was alive with joy."

Dewey, the Small-Town Library Cat Who Touched the World by Vicki Myron and Bret Witter

Are male or female cats more affectionate?

Many cat owners claim that one gender or the other tends to be more affectionate, but there is no evidence that either male or female cats are more cuddly or aloof overall. However, age is a factor because older cats tend to be more affectionate than younger cats. Hormones also play a role, as cats that have been spayed or neutered usually have a stronger bond with their owners because their focus is no longer on roaming, fighting, and mating.

Helix enjoying a belly rub, Jennifer Copley

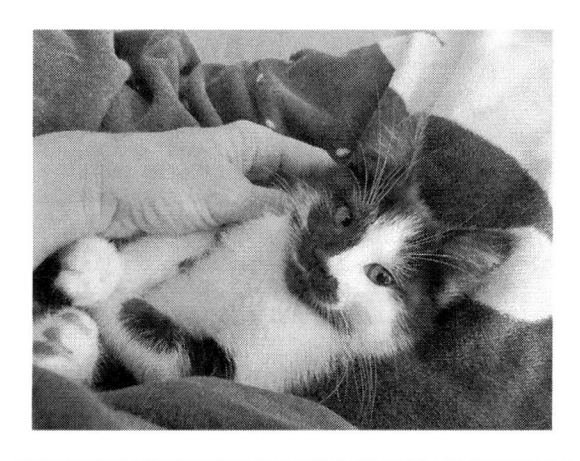

Picatso learning to trust, Jennifer Copley

Reference: Tittle Moore, C. (1999). "Getting a Cat." Fanciers.com.

How can I encourage an aloof cat to be more affectionate?

Frightened feral foster kittens Ash and Aurora, Jennifer Copley

Aloof cats dislike being picked up, refuse to sit on people's laps, and don't spontaneously seek cuddles and pats. A formerly affectionate cat that suddenly becomes aloof may be suffering from a medical problem or reacting to a stressful event, whereas a cat that has always been under-attached was probably poorly socialized as a kitten, has a naturally detached personality, or both.

It's beneficial to engage in gentle handling of kittens starting at around 2 weeks of age. Kittens that were not handled regularly or were handled roughly are more likely to be aloof as adults.

Unless they were mistreated as kittens, aloof cats are usually quite happy with their lives, but their owners may feel rejected and want to establish a stronger bond.

How to bond with an aloof cat

There are a number of things you can do to enhance the bond with an under-attached cat. In some cases, it's possible to make the cat more affectionate. Not all cats have it in them to become cuddlers or lap cats, but the following approaches can improve a human-cat relationship:

- Instead of 1 or 2 big meals per day, feed your cat more frequent smaller meals or healthy treats (assuming the cat is not overweight or on a restricted diet) to increase positive contact.
- Talk to the cat while preparing his food. Stroke him while placing the food on the floor and when he begins to eat so that he'll associate being petted with the positive experience of eating.
- If the cat has a favourite place, sit there and encourage him to come over. If he comes, reward him with a treat while petting him.
- Engage in interactive play with a string or wand toy rather than trying to force the cat to cuddle.
- Try a little catnip – timid cats often come out of their shells and detached cats sometimes become friendlier under its influence.

Don't chase your cat around the house and attempt to force affection on him. This approach usually backfires, making the cat even more avoidant. Only pick him up and hold him if he's cooperating; let him go as soon as he starts to struggle (very young kittens are the exception to this rule; they are more adaptable, so if you hold them gently but firmly, most will calm down, settle in, and become comfortable with handling).

It may be possible to build up a cat's tolerance for being held by calling him over for treats or food, picking him up briefly, and then rewarding him directly afterward, extending the holding time as he grows more comfortable with the procedure.

A frightened feral foster kitten named Golden learns to trust, Jennifer Copley

Reference: Bower, J., & Bower, C. (1998). *The Cat Owner's Problem Solver*. Pleasantville, NY: Reader's Digest Association, Inc./Andromeda Oxford Limited.

Chapter 2: Intelligence

Tyax hanging out in a bookshelf, Jennifer Copley

Are cats intelligent?

Nova photobombs a picture of resident cat Freya, Jennifer Copley

Like people, cats show substantial variation in intelligence. Smart cats demonstrate their intelligence by showing an interest in the world around them, applying various strategies to achieve their goals, learning from past experience, and communicating with humans and other pets.

Curiosity

The old expression "curiosity killed the cat" begs the question, why would an animal lacking in intelligence, driven purely by instinct, endanger her own life just to learn about an unfamiliar object or situation that caught her interest? Why should she show an interest in objects and situations that don't have any direct bearing on her survival? This is a very human thing to do, as many people have risked their lives to satisfy their curiosity.

Much like human children, kittens achieve a higher level of intelligence if they have a stimulating environment where they are handled and played with regularly and encounter many different types of objects and people – in other words, an environment that promotes curiosity and learning.

Learning from experience and practice

Cats may appear unable to learn, but in many cases, it's just that the subject matter doesn't interest them. Cats learn from experience when they find the information relevant, which is why they can develop phobias quite easily. After a single traumatic experience such as being roughly handled by a certain type of person (i.e., a child), the cat may subsequently avoid that category of person completely.

Sage shows an interest in Starbug, Jennifer Copley

Cats are good at remembering useful information (such as noises they have made that achieved the desired response from their owners), and they can recognize the people and animals they have interacted with. Cats can learn their owners' schedules as well, and some act as alarm clocks, attempting to wake their human companions if they sleep past the usual time. Hunting is also a learned behaviour. Unless a kitten is taught how to hunt by his mother, he may never learn how to do it properly.

Cats can learn a variety of additional behaviours if they have patient teachers, including:

- Begging
- Coming when called
- Eating using their paws to pick up the food
- Fetching or catching objects
- Hiding food in a box
- Jumping through hoops
- Leaping at targets
- Meowing on command
- Opening doors
- Playing dead
- Playing simple notes on a piano

- Rolling over
- Running obstacle courses
- Shaking hands
- Sitting on command
- Using a human toilet
- Using a litter box
- Using a scratch post
- Walking on a leash

However, owners shouldn't attempt to train cats in the same way they would train dogs or use negative reinforcement strategies. Cats don't respond well to punishment or sharp vocal tones, which just make them aggressive or fearful. Instead, owners should use rewards and clicker training.

Helix captures a rapidly spinning toy above, Jennifer Copley

Problem solving

Many cat owners have noticed how hard their pets will work to attain a desired goal. They try multiple strategies, rejecting an approach that proves ineffective and trying something new rather than doing the same thing over and over again.

Some cats solve problems by observing humans. For example, a cat may watch a person open a door by turning the handle and later jump up on a nearby object and attempt to turn the handle with his paws. If there is a doorknob rather than a handle, such attempts are inevitably thwarted by a lack of opposable thumbs, but the fact that a cat would try this strategy shows intelligence.

Nimbus and Rambler learn to use a scratcher, Jennifer Copley

Communication

Some cats are more vocal than others, but all cats communicate. Feline communication may involve anything from cheerfully greeting an owner when he arrives home from work to asking for food to expressing anxiety about a situation.

Seymour requests attention, Jennifer Copley

Navigation skills

Cats have impressive memories, so they can usually find their way home after travelling long distances. In addition to relying on memory, they navigate using the angle of the sun (which can be done even on cloudy days using polarized light for wayfinding) and the Earth's magnetic fields (attaching a magnet to a cat will disrupt his navigational skills).

The phenomenal feline navigational ability was demonstrated by Howie the Persian, who crossed 1,000 miles of Australian outback to find his family. Howie had been left in the care of his owner's grandparents while she went on an overseas trip, but he disappeared from their home and showed up a year later on his owner's doorstep. After cleaning the filthy, skinny, injured animal, she realized that it was Howie. He had fought his way back through a vast expanse of harsh desert wilderness to return to the family he loved.

Curious Falcio, Jennifer Copley

A wandering beach cat stopped to hang out with me by the ocean for awhile, Jennifer Copley

A friendly cat pauses on her journey to say hello, Jennifer Copley

References

- Canfield, J., Hansen, M.V., Becker, M., & Kline, C. (1999). *Chicken Soup for the Cat and Dog Lover's Soul*. Deerfield Beach, FL: Health Communications Inc.
- Schneck, M., & Caravan, J. (1990). *Cat Facts*. New York, NY: Barnes & Noble Inc.

Which cat breeds are the most intelligent?

Sphynx, Heikki Siltala, Catza.net, Creative Commons 3.0

Animal Planet has ranked the majority of better-known cat breeds by intelligence, giving each breed a score out of 10. Unfortunately, the criteria for this ranking system are unclear and there is no reliable intelligence test for cats, so the following rankings are somewhat subjective. There is also significant variation within breeds because each has its share of geniuses and less intelligent individuals, so rankings should be considered averages rather than IQ scores for all members of a breed.

Animal Planet's top-ranked cats for intelligence

The Sphynx, a "hairless" breed that actually has a fine peach fuzz coat like soft suede, was the only cat to receive a 10 out of 10 ranking, and owners rave about the intelligence of this breed. A number of additional breeds received a high 9 out of 10 score, including:

- Balinese (essentially a long-haired Siamese)
- Bengal (a wild Asian Leopard Cat/domestic cat cross)
- Colourpoint Shorthair (a breed developed from the Siamese and American and British Shorthairs)
- Havana Brown (a cross of the Siamese and black British or American Shorthairs)
- Javanese (an Oriental Shorthair-Balinese cross)
- Oriental (developed from numerous breeds, including the Siamese)
- Siamese (a naturally occurring breed)

All of the breeds with very high intelligence ratings are derived from the Siamese except for the Bengal, a wild-domestic hybrid. Although there is no doubt that Siamese cats tend to be very bright, cat breeder Norman Auspitz notes that the breeds considered most intelligent also tend to be among the most active, which indicates a bias toward rating more energetic cats higher on intelligence scales.

Balinese, Heikki Siltala, Catza.net, Creative Commons 3.0

Havana, Heikki Siltala, Catza.net, Creative Commons 3.0

Bengal, Heikki Siltala, Catza.net, Creative Commons 3.0

Oriental Shorthair, Heikki Siltala, Catza.net, Creative Commons 3.0

Colourpoint Shorthair, Jennifer Copley

Siamese, Heikki Siltala, Catza.net, Creative Commons 3.0

Cat breeds ranked as very bright

Other breeds that scored in the relatively high range for intelligence (8 out of 10) on the Animal Planet scale included:

- Burmese
- Chartreux
- Devon Rex
- Egyptian Mau
- Japanese Bobtail
- Korat
- Norwegian Forest Cat
- Russian Blue
- Siberian
- Singapura
- Tonkinese
- Turkish Angora
- Turkish Van

Chartreux, Heikki Siltala, Catza.net, Creative Commons 3.0

Burmese, Heikki Siltala, Catza.net, Creative Commons 3.0

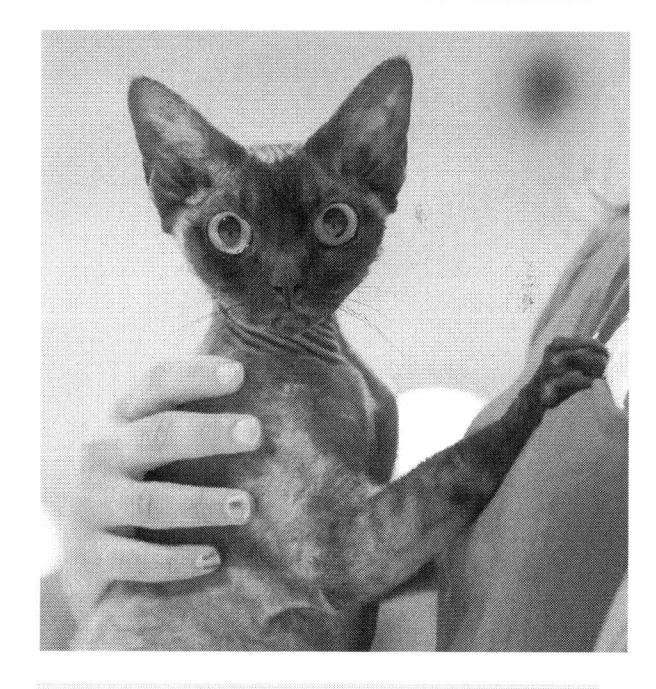

Devon Rex, Heikki Siltala, Catza.net, Creative Commons 3.0

Egyptian Mau, Heikki Siltala, Catza.net, Creative Commons 3.0

Korat, Heikki Siltala, Catza.net, Creative Commons 3.0

Japanese Bobtail, Heikki Siltala, Catza.net, Creative Commons 3.0

Norwegian Forest Cat, Heikki Siltala, Catza.net, Creative Commons 3.0

Russian Blue, Heikki Siltala, Catza.net, Creative Commons 3.0

Singapura, Heikki Siltala, Catza.net, Creative Commons 3.0

Siberian, Heikki Siltala, Catza.net, Creative Commons 3.0

Tonkinese, Angela Thomas, Flickr, Creative Commons 2.0

Turkish Van, Heikki Siltala, Catza.net, Creative Commons 3.0

Turkish Angora, Heikki Siltala, Catza.net, Creative Commons 3.0

Cat breeds that received a respectable ranking of 7 out of 10 included:

- Abyssinian
- American Curl
- American Wirehair
- British Shorthair
- Cornish Rex
- Cymric
- Maine Coon
- Manx
- Ragdoll
- Scottish Fold
- Snowshoe
- Somali

Among these mid-to-high-range cats there are plenty of naturally occurring breeds that arose in various geographical locations and adapted well to local conditions, and a few that resulted from mutations, such as the Scottish Fold and American Curl.

American Curl, Heikki Siltala, Catza.net, Creative Commons 3.0

Abyssinian, Heikki Siltala, Catza.net, Creative Commons 3.0

Cornish Rex, Heikki Siltala, Catza.net, Creative Commons 3.0

British Shorthair, Heikki Siltala, Catza.net, Creative Commons 3.0

Manx, Heikki Siltala, Catza.net, Creative Commons 3.0

American Wirehair, Heikki Siltala, Catza.net, Creative Commons 3.0

Maine Coon, Heikki Siltala, Catza.net, Creative Commons 3.0

Cymric, Heikki Siltala, Catza.net, Creative Commons 3.0

Somali, Heikki Siltala, Catza.net, Creative Commons 3.0

Ragdoll, Heikki Siltala, Catza.net, Creative Commons 3.0

Snowshoe, Heikki Siltala, Catza.net, Creative Commons 3.0

Scottish Fold, Heikki Siltala, Catza.net, Creative Commons 3.0

Cat breeds ranked mid-range to low for intelligence

Several additional breeds just barely made it onto the top half of the intelligence scale, with rankings of 6 out of 10:

- American Shorthair
- Birman
- Bombay

Of course, many fans of these breeds would argue with these rankings. A Google search turns up plenty of articles in which these cats are described as very intelligent.

American Shorthair, Heikki Siltala, Catza.net, Creative Commons 3.0

Bombay, Heikki Siltala, Catza.net, Creative Commons 3.0

Birman, Heikki Siltala, Catza.net, Creative Commons 3.0

The Persian fared even worse with a rating of just 4 out of 10, although the unofficial holder of the "Smartest Cat in the World" title is a Persian named Cuty Boy who has made newspaper headlines for his apparent ability to solve mathematical problems and understand 8 languages.

Persian cat, Heikki Siltala, Catza.net, Creative Commons 3.0

The bottom-rated cats on the Animal Planet scale are the Exotic Shorthair and the Himalayan, which received scores of just 3 out of 10. Both breeds are derived from the Persian, though the Himalayan is also a Siamese cross. It's impossible to determine whether these breeds are truly less intelligent, or raters are simply mistaking docility for dullness.

Exotic Shorthair, Heikki Siltala, Catza.net, Creative Commons 3.0

Himalayan, Joseph Morris, Flickr, Creative Commons 2.0

Problems with ranking cat breeds by intelligence

Are more curious, active cats more intelligent, or is this simply an anthropomorphic bias? Because there is no good test of cat intelligence, it's impossible to say.

Cats apply their intelligence to problems relevant to cats rather than those that interest humans, so feline intelligence remains an elusive concept, and because most cats are not cooperative research subjects, it's difficult to assess their problem-solving abilities.

References

- Animal Planet. (2011). "Cat Breed Selector." Animal.Discovery.com.
- Auspitz, N. (17 December 2005). "Cat Intelligence." En.AllExperts.com.
- Unnithan, S. (23 May 2010). "Purrs of Meaning." *The Hindu*, Cutyboy.com.

Which are smarter: cats or dogs?

Kitten and Beagle, Claudio Matsuoka, Flickr, Creative Commons 2.0

Are dogs smarter than cats, or are cats more intelligent than dogs? Recent studies provide some insights.

Information processing capacity

Dogs have bigger brains than cats (Schultz & Dunbar, 2010), but brain size is not a good indicator of intelligence (Purves et al., 2001), which is evident in the fact that Neanderthals actually had larger brains than modern humans (Braun, 2008). However, the number of neurons in the brain is correlated with intelligence. One study found that cats have 300 million neurons compared to 160 million for dogs (Roth & Dicke, 2005); another found that dogs have between 429 million and 530 million cortical neurons compared to 250 million for cats (Jardim-Messeder et al., 2014). Counts may change again with subsequent studies.

For comparison, a human has around 16 billion cortical neurons (Herculano-Houzel, 2009) and a long-finned pilot whale has 37.2 billion (Mortensen et al., 2014).

Although information processing capacity is important, it's not the only indicator of intelligence.

Comprehension

Smart dogs show an impressive level of understanding. They are able to follow pointing gestures made by humans and use their own gazes to bring objects or situations to the attention of their owners (Douglas, 2009).

Although evidence suggests that cats are cognitively similar to dogs (for example, they are equally capable of using human pointing gestures as a cue to locate food), because most cats are neither motivated nor compliant when participating in research, it's difficult to gauge their understanding (Miklósi et al., 2005). However, cats performed similarly to dogs in a recent study of responses to human facial expressions, gestures, and emotions (Briggs, 2017).

Problem solving ability

Dogs have been studied far more than cats, and cats don't make good research subjects, given their lack of motivation to please, so not much is known about their problem-solving abilities. However, the problem-solving abilities of dogs may also be difficult to determine because they tend to rely on their owners to take a leadership role. Canines often look to humans to solve logistical problems rather than taking the initiative, which may cause them to perform poorly on problem-solving tasks unless their owners encourage them (Douglas, 2009).

Research has shown that a subordinate dog will usually perform better after witnessing another dog engaging in the desired problem-solving behaviour, and that both subordinate and dominant dogs do better after watching a human solve the problem. This illustrates the importance of the dominance hierarchy in canine learning and performance (Pongrácz et al., 2007).

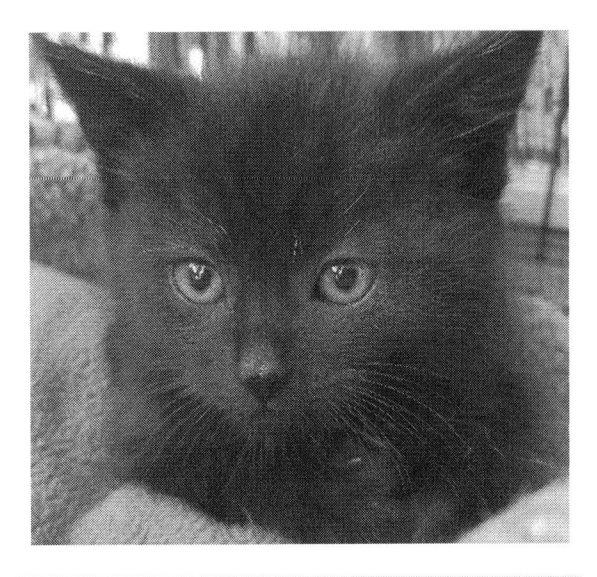

Kylo contemplates the mysteries of the universe, Jennifer Copley

Communication

Cats don't usually meow to other cats and adult wolves rarely bark, so it's likely that companion animal vocalizations evolved as a way to communicate with humans (and may therefore be an indicator of social intelligence). Canines have more vocal flexibility for pitch, frequency, range, length, and tonality, so they are better able to communicate their feelings and intentions (Douglas, 2005), but studies have shown that cat vocalizations have some interesting and unusual features.

Cats can purr at a frequency that has a subliminal effect similar to that of a human baby's cry. This purr, known as the "solicitation purr," which is slightly different from the regular purr, is used to ask for food (McComb et al., 2009). There is also evidence that purring provides pain relief and speeds the healing process (Lyons, 2006).

Memory

Japanese researchers who conducted memory tests with cats and dogs found no significant differences in their abilities (Briggs, 2017).

Perception

Both cats and dogs have far better senses of hearing and smell than humans, but a cat can hear sounds ranging from 45-64,000 hertz, whereas a dog can only hear within a range of 67-45,000. Also, the average cat has more scent receptors than the average dog (some dog breeds, such as the bloodhound, are exceptions to this rule). In addition, cats have an edge over dogs when it comes to night vision, though dogs can see better in low light than humans (Douglas, 2005). The well-developed senses of cats may explain why they often appear to see, hear, or smell things that people (and even dogs) can't perceive.

Intelligence varies among individual animals

It's difficult to determine how intelligent cats and dogs are because in natural settings, they apply their intelligence to problems that are important to cats and dogs, rather than those of interest to humans. Those who spend time with many cats or dogs will notice that some are more intelligent than others. Each species has its geniuses and its duller members. The smartest dog is probably far more intelligent than the dullest cat and vice versa because individual animals vary widely based on genetics, experience, and other factors.

References

- Braun, D. (9 September 2008). "Neanderthal Brain Size at Birth Sheds Light on Human Evolution." Newswatch.National Geographic.com.
- Briggs, H. (2017). "Cats May Be as Intelligent as Dogs, Say Scientists." *BBC News*, January 25.

- Douglas, K. (9 December 2009). "Dogs vs. Cats: The Great Pet Showdown." *New Scientist*.
- Herculano-Houzel, S. (2009). "The Human Brain in Numbers: A Linearly Scaled-Up Primate Brain." *Frontiers in Human Neuroscience. 3*, 31
- Jardim-Messeder, D., et al. (2017). "Dogs Have the Most Neurons, Though Not the Largest Brain: Trade-Off Between Body Mass and Number of Neurons in the Cerebral Cortex of Large Carnivoran Species." *Frontiers in Neuroanatomy, 11*, 118.
- Knapton, S. (2017). "The Truth About Cats and Dogs – Dogs Are Smarter, Say Scientists." *The Guardian*, Nov. 30.
- Lyons, L. (3 April 2006). "Why Do Cats Purr." *Scientific American*, ScientificAmerican.com.
- McComb, K., et al. (2009). "The Cry Embedded Within the Purr." *Current Biology, 19*(13).
- Miklósi, Á., et al. (2005). "A Comparative Study of the Use of Visual Communicative Signals in Interactions Between Dogs (*Canis Familiaris*) and Humans and Cats (*Felis Catus*) and Humans." *Journal of Comparative Psychology, 119*(2), 179-186.
- Mortensen, H.S., et al. "Quantitative Relationships in Delphinid Neocortex." *Frontiers in Neuroanatomy*, 8, 132.
- Pongrácz, P., et al. (2008). "How Does Dominance Rank Status Affect Individual and Social Learning Performance in the Dog (*Canis Familiaris*)?" *Animal Cognition, 11*: 75-82.
- Purves, D., et al. (2001). "'Planning Neurons' in the Monkey Frontal Cortex." *Neuroscience*, 2nd Ed.
- Roth, G., & Dicke, U. (2005). "Evolution of the Brain and Intelligence." *Trends in Cognitive Science, 9*(5): 250-257
- Shultz, S., & Dunbar, R. (2010). "Encephalization Is Not a Universal Macroevolutionary Phenomenon in Mammals but Is Associated with Sociality." *Proceedings of the National Academy of Sciences*, 2010.

Whirly, one of the smartest kittens we've ever fostered, Jennifer Copley

Chapter 3: Anger, Fear, and Anxiety

A frightened feral kitten named Aurora, Jennifer Copley

Why do cats hiss?

A terrified foster kitten named Golden, hissing defensively on her first day with us (fortunately, we were able to win her trust and she became a very affectionate, loving little cat), Jennifer Copley

Cats hiss at those they want to drive away – other animals or people. Young kittens can hiss even before their eyes have opened, which indicates that the behaviour is innate rather than learned.

Hissing is a threatening gesture that causes potential attackers to associate the cat with a poisonous snake. A hissing cat flattens her ears, creating a snakelike face shape, and with her fur standing on end and her back arched, she appears larger and more capable of inflicting damage.

Cats aren't the only creatures that use mimicry this way. There are many non-poisonous insects that have markings similar to those of poisonous species to trick potential predators into thinking that it would be far too risky to take a bite. Insects may also mimic less tasty or faster moving species that are difficult to catch. Some butterflies and fish also have markings that resemble eyes on areas other than their heads to trick predators into biting the wrong spot so they can escape.

Reference: Morris, D. (1997). *Cat World: A Feline Encyclopedia*. New York, NY: Viking Adult.

Why do some cats attack when being petted?

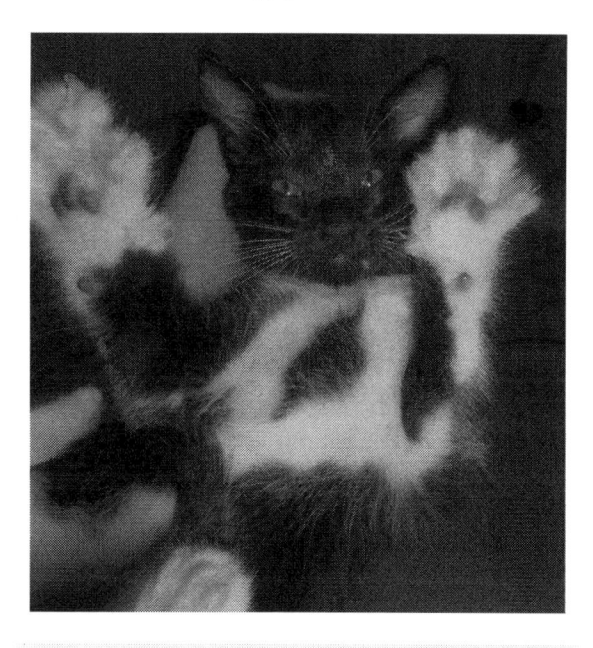

A playful foster kitten, Jennifer Copley

Some cats switch to attack mode while being stroked because they:

- Experience over-stimulation of the nerves where fur meets skin
- Are irritated by a build-up of static electricity caused by petting
- Are stressed due to recent changes in the household or other problems
- Have medical issues that make being touched on certain spots painful
- Were taken away from their mothers and littermates too early
- Did not experience sufficient interaction with humans during the critical socialization period as kittens
- Fall asleep while being petted, wake up suddenly, and panic before they realize what's going on
- Have a need to control the situation either to feel secure or to assert dominance

Overstimulation or skin irritation

Cats have very sensitive skin. While some cats can soak up affection indefinitely, others rapidly become over-stimulated and can only manage a short session of petting or grooming. When a cat becomes over-stimulated or experiences the extreme discomfort caused by a build-up of static electricity, he reflexively lashes out.

Petting aggression is not a personal slight. The cat may really like the person who is stroking him and probably feels no anger toward that individual. He's reacting to the discomfort, and the behaviour is just a reflex.

Medical or psychological problems

There are a number of medical problems that may cause a cat to lash out when being petted due to pain. These include arthritis, parasite infestation, inflammatory polyps, dental issues, hip dysplasia, and a variety of other conditions. Whenever a formerly calm cat begins acting aggressively, a full veterinary check-up is recommended to rule out medical problems.

Cats may also be oversensitive due to psychological stress. Common stressors that cats experience include:

- Moving to a new home
- Arrival of a new baby or another pet
- Bullying by a resident pet or neighbourhood animal
- Rough handling by members of the household

Lack of early socialization

There is a critical period in a kitten's development during which he learns when to react with aggression, as well as the appropriate level of force to use in any given situation. Kittens that are orphaned or removed from their mothers and siblings too early miss out on these lessons, so they are more likely to swat or bite rather than just warning a person away with hostile body language.

A cat may also become aggressive when petted because his interactions with humans during the critical period for socialization (the first few months of life) were unpleasant or non-existent. Rough handling during this time can lead to ambivalent behaviour because the cat wants to trust but becomes fearful in a vulnerable position.

Other causes of petting aggression

Some experts believe that certain cats become aggressive after a few strokes because they have a need to control the situation. Just as a person wouldn't want to be forcibly hugged for too long, being petted for a length of time defined by a human may feel oppressive to some cats, particularly if they're insecure or have a high need for dominance.

Each cat has unique petting preferences, and some are far more sensitive than others. Some cats are happier with scratches behind their ears or on their chins than full-body petting. Other cats love to be stroked, but need a break after a few seconds, and some cats will happily absorb affection all day long.

When a cat is prone to petting aggression, his human companions should learn to recognize the signs of over-stimulation and teach children to recognize them as well. Early warning signs include:

- Tail twitching
- Body stiffening
- Skin Rippling
- Pupils dilating
- Ears flattening
- Claws unsheathing
- Low growl

If any of these behaviours occur, stop stroking the cat until he has calmed down and appears receptive to affection.

The petting threshold of an overly sensitive cat can often be increased with positive reinforcement, such as offering favourite foods while petting him, after every stroke or two. On the other hand, a cat's petting threshold will be decreased if he's punished for reflexively engaging in petting aggression. Punishment nearly always increases aggression in cats rather than decreasing it.

Adult cat preferences tend to be stable over time. Those who want cats they can pet for hours on end should spend plenty of time holding and stroking prospective adoptees to find cats that meet their needs. Spending time together beforehand increases the likelihood of getting a good personality match.

References

- BC SPCA. (n.d.). "Petting Aggression: Does Your Cat Suddenly Attack You During Petting?" ASPCA.org.
- Nash, H., DVM, MS, Veterinary Services Department, Drs. Foster & Smith. (2009). "Petting-Related Aggression in Cats." PetEducation.com.

Why do cats fight?

Foster kittens Nimbus and Rambler playfighting on my lap, Jennifer Copley

There are many reasons why cats suddenly puff up, hiss, growl, chase, or attack one another. Types of cat aggression include:

- Defensive/fearful: A fight-or-flight response
- Inter-male: Fighting over females and associated territories
- Misdirected: Aimed at something other than the irritant
- Non-recognition: Mistaking a friend for a stranger
- (Indoor) territorial: Day-to-day maintenance of and challenges to the social hierarchy
- Playfighting: A normal behaviour whereby kittens practice their fighting skills with one another

Defensive/fearful aggression

If a cat feels threatened, particularly if she's backed into a corner or a wall and doesn't have a good escape route, she may go into a defensive posture, puffing up, hissing, and growling. If the harasser doesn't back off, she may feel that she has no other choice than to attack. Cats displaying defensive aggression are unlikely to pursue if the other animal or person retreats.

Cats may also attack humans who punish them because they feel a constant sense of threat from those people, and they will be aggressive toward other animals that try to dominate them, harm them, or take over the household if they don't keep them in line. A cat may also be aggressive if he suffers from severe generalized anxiety or has recently experienced a trauma that has made him unusually fearful.

If a cat is afraid of a new person or animal, keeping the feared individual at a distance and rewarding the cat with food or treats when that person or animal is visible but safely on the other side of the room can help to mitigate the fear. If the problem is another animal, the feared cat or dog should be on a leash, behind a baby gate, or in a wire cage while the fearful cat has the opportunity to grow comfortable and learn to associate the positive experience of food with the feared individual.

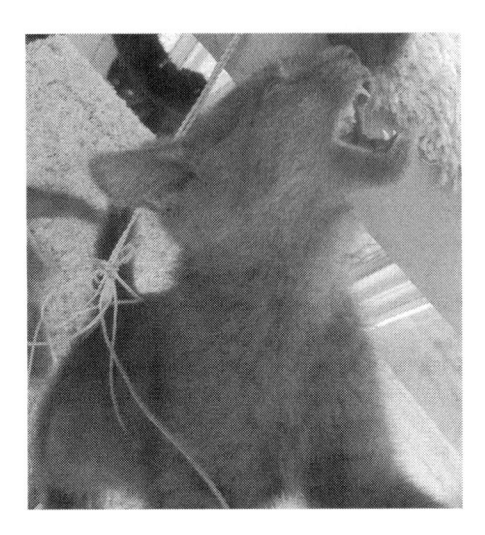

A playfully aggressive foster kitten named Hadron, Jennifer Copley

Inter-male aggression

Fighting among unneutered male cats is often the most violent type of feline aggression. In addition to the potential for injury and abscesses at puncture wound sites, cats that engage in damaging fights are at greater risk for acquiring feline leukemia (FeLV) and feline immunodeficiency virus (FIV). Neutering male cats can decrease fighting by 90% as well as reducing the number of health problems a cat is likely to suffer later in life.

A minor fight between 2 young male foster kittens, TJ and Callahan, Jennifer Copley

Misdirected aggression

Much like people, cats will sometimes take their anger out on whoever is available rather than the person, animal, or object that provoked it. A cat may attack a human, another cat, the family dog, or even a random household object because she's seen a cat outside that she doesn't like but can't reach. If a cat regularly gets angry in response to seeing unwelcome animals outdoors, keeping the blinds shut or curtains drawn can help.

Fear-induced aggression can also be misdirected, as when a loud noise causes one startled cat to attack another because his fight-or-flight response has been triggered and he has to do something with all that adrenaline. While scary events are the most likely cause of misdirected aggression, something unfamiliar or annoying may also trigger it.

Foster kittens practice their fighting skills, Jennifer Copley

Non-recognition aggression

Cats recognize people and animals primarily through their sense of smell, and if the smell changes, a cat may believe that his roommate is an invader. This can happen when one cat goes away, either to a groomer or the veterinarian, and picks up a different set of odours.

Non-recognition aggression can be prevented by taking the cat that has just come home into a separate room and closing the door to keep him away from other household cats until he has time to groom himself and pick up familiar household smells again. Taking a dry, clean cloth, rubbing it gently over other household cats, and then rubbing the returning cat with it to transfer the scents can also help to smooth the reintroduction.

(Indoor) territorial aggression

Sometimes a cat will be aggressive if she feels that another cat is invading her territory, even if she used to consider that cat a buddy. Adolescent and young adult cats (around 5-10 months of age) are more likely to challenge dominant feline roommates by staring at them or even growling or hissing, eventually progressing to chasing and attack. The targeted roommate may respond aggressively, and both combatants may also engage in passive-aggressive behaviour such as spraying or hogging the food bowls.

Territorial issues are most likely to occur when a new cat enters the scene. Providing each cat with his own food and water bowls and litter box can help to reduce territorial aggression.

A defensive fight position, Jennifer Copley

An epic kitten Fight Club takedown, Jennifer Copley

Chili starts a fight with Lily, Jennifer Copley

Falcio leaps backward to avoid Kest's takedown attempt

Reference: Rainbolt, D. (2008). *Cat Wrangling Made Easy: Maintaining Peace & Sanity in Your Multicat Home.* Guilford, CT: The Lyons Press.

How can I prevent cat fights?

A foster kitten bites his brother's neck, Jennifer Copley

Batting at things or tackling moving objects is normal behaviour for cats. If your cat pounces on you or other members of the household, she may just be bored and require more interactive playtime, but unprovoked hissing, growling, scratching, and biting can indicate a problem.

Underlying causes of cat aggression

Cats may be aggressive because they were not properly socialized as kittens or because they have been mistreated. Some cats are aggressive because they have inherited the tendency from a parent, and some people train their cats to be aggressive without realizing it. Encouraging a kitten to pounce on your feet and bite your toes or tackle your wiggling hands may be cute, but when an adult cat does this, someone could end up in the hospital with an infected bite wound.

Cats may also become aggressive due to pain or anxiety. Bring your cat in for a veterinary check-up to rule out medical problems before attempting other treatments for aggression, particularly if a formerly mellow cat starts behaving aggressively toward other pets or people.

Feline conflicts in multi-cat households

Cats that are otherwise good friends may have a little spat from time to time and this isn't anything to be concerned about, but serious conflicts should be addressed before they escalate. In some cases, a bully and victim relationship may develop, or one cat may become a social pariah in a multi-cat household. These silent conflicts can be identified by observing feline interactions. The aggressor:

- Stares directly at the other cat
- Blocks the other cat from accessing resources such as food or prime sleeping spots
- Stalks the victim with head held low and hindquarters elevated (fur may be puffed up as well)
- Growls at the other cat
- May spray or urinate outside the litter box to assert territorial claims

The cat that feels threatened or intimidated may:

- Avoid eye contact with the more assertive cat
- Spend a lot of time hiding
- Back off and let other cats access food or desirable sleeping spots
- Crouch low and then run away when encountering a more aggressive cat
- Spray or urinate outside the litter box to mark territory
- Urinate or defecate outside the litter box because he is too afraid to leave his hiding place, or another cat has attacked him while he was using the box
- Attack another cat in the household, passing the aggression along
- Suffer from health problems such as cystitis

Preventing fights between cats

To prevent cat fights and related problems such as urine marking:

- Avoid competition over resources by providing a litter box, food bowls, water dishes, cat beds,

- and toys for each cat so they don't have to share.
- Place resources such as feeding stations and litter boxes at different locations around the house so the threatened cat can eat and eliminate in peace.
- Place a litter box in an area where the fearful cat can escape easily so he won't feel cornered when using it.
- Provide "kitty condos" (cardboard, wooden, or plastic boxes with cat-sized doorway holes and some bedding inside), cat trees with high perches, and other places to escape, hide, and claim as personal territory.
- Have all cats spayed or neutered.

Fights are most likely to occur when new cats are added to the household, but there are strategies that can be used to help new pets grow calm and comfortable with resident pets and vice versa. These include desensitization, conditioning, and reinforcement.

Desensitization requires allowing animals to gradually become accustomed first to their respective scents and then to seeing each other. This can be done by feeding the cats on either side of a closed door until they are comfortable in each other's presence.

Conditioning is associating one thing with another. For example, if you provide your cat's favourite food whenever she's in the same room as the animal or person to whom she shows aggression, she will associate that individual with the positive experience of eating. When using this strategy, ensure that other people and animals keep a respectful distance and don't bother the cat while she eats.

Reinforcement involves providing rewards (which can be anything from verbal praise to pats to treats) when the cat curbs her aggressive response. When she's in a room with the person or animal that provokes her hostility, you can first calm her down by petting her and speaking in a soothing voice, and then offer the reward when she's behaving calmly.

Punishment, physical or verbal, actually increases fear and aggression in cats, so it should be avoided. A cat that is punished in the presence of the animal or person to whom she shows aggression will associate that individual with the negative experience, and her hostility will increase. If your cat is scratching or biting, you can grab her gently by the scruff of the neck to pull her away and say "no," but anything more forceful, such as hitting or shouting, will make the situation worse in the long term.

There are medications to treat anxiety and aggression in cats, but they should be used only as a last resort because they can have side effects and cats may become addicted to tranquillizing anti-anxiety medications such as benzodiazepines. Medication is usually given for just a few months, though in some cases it's required for more than a year.

Note: although cats respond to many of the same medications as those used to treat anxiety and depression in humans, they require much smaller amounts – a human-sized dose of medication can be lethal to a cat, so you should never give your cat medication unless recommended by a veterinarian.

A foster kitten behaves with defensive aggressiveness the first time she sees her reflection in a mirror, Jennifer Copley

References

- Merck & Co., Inc., Eds. Cynthia M. Kahn, BA, MA, & Scott Line, DVM, PhD, Dipl ACVB. (2007). *The Merck/Merial Manual for Pet Health, Home Edition*.
- Whiteley, E., Dr. (2008). "How to Solve Cat Behaviour Problems." HowStuffWorks.com.

How can I reduce my cat's separation anxiety?

A foster kitten with an intense stare, Jennifer Copley

Why are some cats so clingy and needy? Feline personalities are shaped by both nature and nurture. Certain cat breeds (such as the Siamese) tend to be more affectionate, whereas others are usually more independent. Not all affectionate cats are clingy, but they may be more likely to develop this trait, particularly when under stress.

Cats with timid, nervous temperaments may become clingy due to specific phobias or the feline equivalent of generalized anxiety disorder. Cats are also likely to develop needy personalities if they have suffered abandonment, deprivation, or poor socialization as kittens.

Symptoms of over-dependence in cats

Clingy cats want to be with their owners constantly. They demand attention frequently and try to maintain physical contact (such as sitting on an owner's lap) as much as possible. They follow their owners around, become distressed when left alone, and may lose their appetites or vomit when their owners leave the house. In some cases, they develop neurotic habits such as:

- Pulling out fur
- Sucking on wool or fabric
- Destructive scratching
- Spraying, urinating, or defecating outside the litter box

If a formerly independent cat suddenly becomes needy, this usually signals a medical problem or anxiety about a specific event, such as:

- The arrival of a new baby or pet
- The death of a beloved animal or person
- Moving house

If a cat that wasn't needy in the past becomes clingy, bring her in for a veterinary check-up to rule out illness. If the clinginess has been triggered by a recent household change, provide extra attention to get her through the rough patch. With a little extra support, most cats eventually return to normal. However, if the clinginess is a long-term problem rather than a temporary reaction, the following approaches can be used to reduce separation anxiety:

- Don't engage in elaborate good-bye routines when leaving the house; have keys ready by the door or in a bag so you can exit quickly.
- Give a favourite toy or treat to the cat just before you leave so that she associates your leaving with something positive.
- When returning home, ignore the cat for 10-15 minutes, especially if she demands attention. Wait until she's calm and then provide affection.
- If the cat engages in undesirable behaviour such as house soiling or scratching furniture while you're out, don't yell or punish her, as this will make stress-induced behaviours worse.
- Provide a hideaway (this can be anything from a fancy carpeted kitty condo to a cardboard box with a doorway cut into it). Add a piece of your clothing (unwashed so that it has your scent on

it) for comfort. This gives the cat a safe place to retreat when she's alone and anxious. A comfort object should also be provided if she needs to stay overnight at the vet's or board somewhere else temporarily.

- A few fake departures can be helpful for teaching your cat not to panic whenever she sees you getting ready to leave. Put on your coat and go out for a minute or two, then come back, varying the length of time until she learns that not every leave-taking means you'll be gone for hours or days.

Eclipse hopes for a treat, Jennifer Copley

How to help needy cats become more independent

To help needy cats become more confident and independent:

- Engage in interactive play rather than cuddling all the time.
- Ignore demanding behaviour. Have one or more set times to dispense affection (such as in the evening with a good book or favourite television show) and stick to those routines.
- If the cat begins to knead or suck on your clothing or earlobes (which are common self-comforting behaviours in needy cats), gently remove her from your lap, get up, and leave the room.
- If she's fixated on a single person, have others share in petting, feeding, playing, and grooming to expand the circle of people with whom she feels comfortable.
- Try a calming feline pheromone product such as Feliway (not all cats respond to it, but many do).
- If she's friendly toward other cats, consider adopting another cat for company, preferably a kitten to reduce the risk of dominance struggles.
- Sometimes neediness results from boredom. Create an enriched environment with plenty of toys, healthy treats hidden around the house (assuming the cat is not overweight), cat trees, cat-safe plants, and an entertaining view (such as a birdfeeder outside a window).
- Owners who are afraid to let their cats out due to traffic, predators, and other hazards should consider putting up a cat fence or enclosure if they have outdoor space so they can let their cats out safely. Leash training and taking the cat out for safe excursions is also an option.

In extreme cases, if all else fails, a veterinarian may prescribe anti-anxiety medication or recommend a natural anxiety remedy.

References

- Christensen, W. (2004). *Outwitting Cats*. Guilford, CT: The Lyons Press.
- Dodman, N. (2010). "Separation Anxiety in Cats." PetPlace.com.
- Feline Advisory Bureau. (n.d.). "Cats and Stress." FabCats.org.
- Hillestad, K. (2010). "Separation Anxiety in Cats." PetEducation.com.
- InfoPet.com. (n.d.). "Cats: Behavioural Problems."
- Plotnick, A. (2006). "Separation Anxiety in Cats." ManhattanCats.com.

Why do some cats become anxious or phobic?

A terrified feral foster kitten (Katerina eventually bonded with us, but it took awhile to win her trust), Jennifer Copley

Generalized anxieties and phobias can manifest in a number of ways. An anxious cat may withdraw from social interaction with other cats or people or become aggressive, hissing and even clawing or biting with little provocation.

Aggression caused by anxiety tends to be defensive and results from fear rather than hostility. A defensive-aggressive cat may have been mistreated as a kitten, or he may be phobic of a specific individual or distressed about a situation such as a new pet or some other major change in the household.

Specific phobias

Aggression toward or avoidance of specific people or animals is usually caused by a phobia rather than generalized anxiety. A cat may become fearful of an individual who has mistreated him, but he may also develop a generalized phobia of a certain type of person (i.e., children, men with facial hair, people wearing hats, etc.).

Kittens that don't encounter many different types of people during the critical socialization period (the first few months of life) are more likely to develop generalized phobias. For example, a kitten that only interacts with female humans may develop a phobia of male humans later on. Also, a cat that has been mistreated may develop a general phobia of all those who resemble the abusive individual in some way.

Anxiety-related litter box avoidance

A cat may regularly urinate or defecate on the floor or furniture rather than using the litter box due to medical problems, generalized anxiety, anxiety related to a specific ongoing situation, or a litter box phobia. Litter box phobias are usually caused by traumatic events while using the box, such as being attacked by another animal or being punished for having an accident and then brought to the box directly afterward.

Other anxiety behaviours

Anxious cats may pull out their fur or overgroom, causing bald patches or sores. However, as with litter box avoidance, these behaviours can indicate medical problems or parasite infestation, so a veterinary checkup is required before assuming the problem is psychological.

A cat that is severely anxious, depressed, or ill may stop eating, drinking, or grooming altogether, though cats may stop eating for other reasons, such as being run off the food bowl by another pet or not wanting to eat because the food is in a noisy, high-traffic area of the house.

Because failure to eat, drink, or groom can be signs of a serious medical problem, consult a veterinarian to rule out medical conditions before assuming the cause is psychological. Cats that stop drinking should receive medical care quickly, as they can become dangerously dehydrated.

Anxiety treatments

There are a number of effective treatments for anxiety and related behavioural problems. Spending more quality time with the anxious cat and identifying and eliminating sources of distress will often solve the problem. However, it's not always possible to remove a stressor. A veterinarian-prescribed anti-anxiety medication can be used as a last resort, but most anxiety problems can be treated with behavioural therapies such as desensitization (gradual, supported exposure to the individual, thing, or situation that is feared) and conditioning (providing treats or praise and affection in the presence of the feared thing to replace negative associations with positive ones).

References

- Fox, M.W. (2007). *Cat Body, Cat Mind*. The Lyons Press.
- Plotnick, A., MS, DVM, ACVIM, ABVP. (2 September 2006). "Hair Loss in Cats." ManhattanCats.com.

An anxious, newly arrived foster kitten, Jennifer Copley

Why are cats afraid of cucumbers?

A few years go the internet was flooded with viral videos of terrified cats leaping away from vegetables. Owners had discovered that if they placed produce items such as cucumbers or bananas behind their unsuspecting pets, when the cats turned around, they would leap into the air or launch preemptive strikes against their imaginary attackers. What accounts for these panicked responses to surprise cucumbers? No one knows for sure, but many believe that cats react badly to cucumbers because their shape makes them look like snakes.

Snake phobias are common in people because this fear gave our ancestors a survival advantage by reducing the risk of poisonous bites, and cats may be phobic of snakes for the same reason. According to the snake theory of feline cucumber panic, snake-shaped vegetables induce an automatic fear response due to natural selection. In other words, cats that were not afraid of poisonous snakes were more likely to die before procreating. However, some people believe that the startle response is triggered by the surprise of seeing something that shouldn't be there rather than a specific fear of snakes, as certain cats have reacted just as fearfully to less snakelike objects such as apples (cats, understandably, don't like anything that seems to sneak up on them). Also, cats hunt snakes in the wild, though their prey are usually smaller reptiles rather than large, poisonous snakes.

While surprise probably plays a role in the terrified responses to unexpected produce, more cats react badly to snake-shaped things than spherical objects such as apples. For example, our cats are wary of coming out on the deck if the garden hose is coiled up there.

Whether the panicked reactions are attributable to a fear of snakes or a more general fear of unexpected things, having a quickly and easily activated startle response significantly increases a cat's likelihood of avoiding predators and territorial attackers. Because the genes of cats that react swiftly to surprising things are favored by natural selection, a sensitive startle response persists in the feline gene pool.

Many owners find it hilarious to frighten their pets with surprise objects, but this is extremely stressful for their cats, and there is a risk that they will be injured if they crash into things or land badly after leaping away from perceived threats. Cats that are frightened (particularly if this occurs on multiple occasions) may also develop generalized anxiety or associative phobias. For example, if someone scares a cat near his litter box, he may avoid it in the future and go in other areas of the house.

While many believe these vegetable pranks are harmless, the effects of pranking may be worse for cats than humans because animals can't understand jokes, so they don't get the relief of realizing that they are not actually in danger. Instead, they remain frightened and bewildered because humans are mocking their distress rather than comforting them for reasons they can't understand.

Pet behaviour experts advise against scaring animals on purpose because of the potential for physical and psychological harm. Repeatedly terrorizing an animal can trigger severe ongoing stress reactions that may suppress the immune system, leading to increased risk of illness and reduced ability to recover from it. Subjecting pets to unnecessary stress can also cause behavioural problems, as anxious cats are more likely to have accidents outside the litter box or behave in a defensively aggressive manner, scratching and biting whenever they feel threatened.

References

- Clark Howard, B. (2015). "People Are Scaring Their Cats with Cucumbers. They Shouldn't." National Geographic, NationalGeographic.com.
- Cornell Feline Health Center. (2016). "Cats and Cucumbers - Our Behavior Expert Talks About Why Cats Are Freaking Out." Cornell University College of Veterinary Medicine, Vet.Cornell.edu.
- Corney, C. (n.d.). "Why Are Cats Scared of Cucumbers." BBC Science Focus Magazine, ScienceFocus.com.
- DiNuzzo, E. (n.d.). "This Is Why Cats Are Afraid of Cucumbers." Reader's Digest, ReadersDigest.ca.
- Valiente, A. (2015). "Why These Scaredy Cats Are Absolutely Terrified of Cucumbers." ABC News, ABCNews.go.com.

Brasti (black and white), a very anxious feral foster kitten, becomes more confident with the help of his friendly, laid back playmate Dari (tabby), as the two kittens develop their fighting skills together with playful sparring, Jennifer Copley

Chapter 4: Communication

A chatty foster kitten, Jennifer Copley

What is my cat trying to tell me when he meows?

Aspen and Merlin in a talkative mood, Jennifer Copley

Cats make nearly 100 different types of vocalizations, which include:

- *Meowing*: Usually only used with people, meowing can mean many things, depending on the volume and intensity (a hello meow is usually quieter than a meow used to request food or to be let outside)
- *Mewing*: Used to identify and/or locate another cat
- *Growling*: A warning to keep your distance
- *Hissing*: A "keep away" defensive sound, designed to scare away an enemy by mimicking the noise a poisonous snake makes before striking
- *Spitting*: A short popping sound, often occurring along with hissing if the cat has been threatened or surprised
- *Screeching or shrieking*: A defensive, aggressive, or outraged sound; may also indicate pain
- *Chirping*: Usually expresses a friendly greeting
- *Trilling*: More musical than chirping; indicates happiness or excitement
- *Chattering*: An excited sound made by a cat that sees a bird or other prey she can't reach
- *Yowling/howling*: Often done by older cats at night to express fright, confusion, disorientation, or anxiousness; un-spayed females that want to attract mates will also yowl
- *Moaning*: A drawn-out, sad noise cats make when they're about to vomit; elderly cats may also moan when disoriented
- *Purring*: Signifies contentment in a healthy cat (cats often purr when sick or injured as well because purring speeds the healing process)

Reference: Hotchner, T. (2007). *The Cat Bible: Everything Your Cat Expects You to Know*. London, UK: Penguin Group.

Let me out! A foster kitten objects to the starter cage (newly arrived kittens have regular cuddle time and are allowed out for supervised runs of the office but they aren't given complete freedom until we've observed them for awhile to ensure that they have no medical problems requiring treatment or dangerous behaviours such as cord chewing, and are using their litter box appropriately), Jennifer Copley

What is my cat saying with her body language?

The Countess Hissyfit reacts to a perplexing sound behind her, Jennifer Copley

To figure out what your cat is saying with her body, look at her overall body position and then the positions of individual body parts:

- *Relaxed, friendly:* Ears point forward, tail is relaxed or upright, whiskers are straight, fur is flat
- *Annoyed:* Tail tip is twitching, whiskers are pulled back so that they are flat against the face, ears are flat against the cat's head
- *Aggressive:* Staring, hair on the tail and back is puffed up, tail thumps the ground or swishes rapidly, lips are curled into a snarl, the cat is facing forward and may have her butt in the air so she can pounce easily
- *Scared:* Hair is raised on the tail and back, tail is either held close to the cat's body or lashing, whiskers are flat against the face, ears are flat against the cat's head, the cat is crouching, pupils are dilated (large)
- *Sick:* Eyes may be half closed, tail is between the legs, ears and/or whiskers may be in odd positions

Your cat's eyes, tail, and ears in particular can tell you a lot about her state of mind.

The eyes

An unblinking stare suggests a challenge or defensiveness. Round pupils may signify interest, excitement, or fear, and a sudden dilation of the pupils may indicate that the cat is ready to launch an attack due to fear or defensiveness. If the cat allows her eyelids to droop or slowly closes her eyes, she is relaxed and trusting.

The Earl of Grey shows mixed emotions, Jennifer Copley

The tail

The following are tail signals that most cats use to communicate:

- *Upright:* Confident and friendly; a greeting or a request for food
- *Question mark shape:* Curious or interested
- *Inverted U:* Defensively aggressive (adult cats); may indicate playfulness in kittens
- *Curled and tucked under the body:* Feeling threatened or wanting to be left alone
- *Slightly flicking:* Indecisive, thinking
- *Flicking suddenly, rapidly:* Anxiety or agitation

- *Flicking constantly:* A critique of something in her surroundings
- *Thumping:* Frustrated or annoyed, may precede an attack
- *Lashing back and forth:* An attack is likely
- *Between the legs:* A submissive posture
- *Straight back and puffy:* Signifies aggression, dominance
- *Pointing downward and puffy:* Indicates fear-based aggression
- *Upright and puffy:* Terror and indecision about whether to launch a pre-emptive strike or maintain a defensive posture (often used by kittens when confronting dogs)
- *Upright and quivering:* May signify an intention to spray, particularly in unfixed males; can also be a friendly greeting or indicate mild excitement
- *Crouching with tail straight behind; tail may be twitching:* Stalking prey, toys, other pets, or people

The question-mark tail position, Jennifer Copley

The ears

The following ear positions and movements provide information about a cat's mood and intentions.

Standing upright and rotated slightly forward

Ears that are "pricked" and pointing forward indicate that the cat is alert and interested in something, and that he feels confident enough to explore the situation. This can be differentiated from the relaxed ear position in which the ears are tilted slightly back.

Cats point their ears forward for activities that require being very alert to incoming sensory information, such as hunting. They may also swivel one or both ears toward an interesting sound, manoeuvring them like satellite dishes.

Flattened backward

Cats flatten their ears when they're feeling defensive. The flatter the ears lie against the skull, the more frightened the cat feels. Additional signs of defensiveness include whiskers flattening against the cheeks and pupils dilating (growing larger). A defensive cat may attack if she's very frightened,

Alert ears, relaxed pupils, and a curious tail, signifying fearless interest, Jennifer Copley

particularly if she's so scared that her fur is standing on end.

If only one ear is flattened, the cat may be feeling ambiguous about a situation. He is concerned about something, but not sure whether fear is warranted.

The alert, interested ear position, Jennifer Copley

Flattened sideways

In the case of a cat-to-cat conflict, it can be difficult for owners to tell which cat is the instigator and which is on the defense because a threatened cat may launch a pre-emptive strike. However, you can usually identify the bully by looking at the ears of the combatants. The more aggressive cat will also have flattened ears, but her ears will usually be rotated to the side rather than straight back.

The body language of the two cats provides additional clues. Like the defensive cat, the aggressive cat will usually have flattened whiskers and dilated pupils, but the defensive cat will minimize her size by crouching or slinking and lowering her tail, whereas the aggressive cat will stand sideways on her tiptoes, arch her back, and puff up her fur to make herself appear bigger and more threatening.

Sustained eye contact can also be a sign of aggression in cats. The dominant cat will stare, whereas the submissive cat will cast her eyes downward, avoiding eye contact.

Foster kittens Tesla (with upright ears) and Tyax (with flattened ears because he was far more frightened than his sister when he arrived), Jennifer Copley

Twitching

Twitching ears often signify frustration or irritation, but if the cat is flicking or twitching his ears frequently and also scratching or pawing at them, this may indicate a medical problem such as infection or parasite infestation.

Sir Shady shows fear with one flattened ear, Jennifer Copley

Sage shows mild concern about something, Jennifer Copley

Kest in the pre-pounce position, Jennifer Copley

Golden shows fear with dilated pupils, Jennifer Copley

Feline music critics: The Earl of Grey and Princess Fluffington react to my singing, Jennifer Copley

Relaxed body language and lack of fur puffing indicate that this is a friendly playfight, Jennifer Copley

References

- Cats International. (2007). "Your Cat's Tail, Ear, and Eye Signals." CatsInternational.org.
- Christensen, W., and the Staff of the Humane Society of the United States. (2002). *The Humane Society of the United States Complete Guide to Cat Care*. New York, NY: St. Martin's Press.
- Dodman, N., Dr. (2009). "What Is Your Cat Saying? Reading Your Cat's Body Language." PetPlace.com.
- Hartwell, S. (2009). "Cat Communication – Body Language." MessyBeast.com.
- Hotchner, T. (2007). *The Cat Bible: Everything Your Cat Expects You to Know*. London: Penguin Group.
- Tabor, R. (1997). *Understanding Cat Behaviour*. Cincinnati, OH: F&W Publications, Inc.
- "Tail Talk." (2006). FelineExpress.com.
- Warner, T. (2007). *Cat Body Language Phrasebook: 100 Ways to Read Their Signals*. San Diego, CA: Salamander Books.

Do cats sulk?

The Countess Hissyfit watches me warily (she was more challenging to win over than most, but eventually came to love us), Jennifer Copley

Many owners think that their cats are giving them the cold shoulder when they turn their backs and avoid eye contact or interaction after being scolded. However, contrary to popular belief, this behaviour doesn't result from wounded pride or a desire to get revenge by giving an owner the silent treatment. This misconception stems from a misunderstanding of feline communication.

When a cat stares at another cat, she's behaving in a dominant manner and challenging her rival. When two cats are locked in a battle for dominance, both may stare because neither wants to show weakness. Eventually, the subordinate cat will look away, conceding victory to the dominant cat. If neither cat looks away, a fight may break out.

Given the size of the owner in comparison to the cat (and the fact that the cat depends on his owner for food), he is likely to view his human companion as more powerful, and therefore dominant. When his human companion is behaving in what the cat perceives as a hostile or aggressive manner (i.e., raising his voice) while staring directly at the cat, the cat feels threatened. He will turn away and avert his eyes to signal submission and avoid provoking further hostility.

This is why scolding or punishing cats is ineffective. The cat perceives these behaviours as threatening and retreats, and the resulting anxiety will often provoke another round of undesirable behaviour rather than preventing it. Positive reinforcement for good behaviour is far more effective.

A shy cat avoids eye contact, Jennifer Copley

Reference: Morris, D. (1987). *Catlore*. London, UK: Jonathan Cape Ltd.

Why do some cats howl, especially at night?

22-year-old resident cat Laya howling, Jennifer Copley

Common causes of howling or loud meowing in cats include medical issues, attention seeking, stress, grief, boredom, feline cognitive dysfunction syndrome, and breed tendency.

Illness

If a formerly quiet cat has begun crying or howling plaintively, this may indicate a medical problem. Cats tend to be stoic; many don't show symptoms until an illness has become quite severe. In such cases, the howling is caused by physical and psychological distress.

When howling starts up suddenly, consult a veterinarian as soon as possible. Medical problems should be ruled out before attributing the behaviour to other causes, particularly if the cat is eating or drinking more or less than usual or has started having accidents outside the litter box. Older cats are prone to kidney disease and hyperthyroidism, both of which may cause howling.

Attention seeking

Many cats learn that talking results in feeding, affection, or some other form of interaction. Cats that are desperate for attention may yell just to get a reaction, even if it's a negative one.

If owners want to discourage chattiness, they shouldn't provide any attention (positive or negative) while cats are vocalizing and spend more quality time with them when they're being quiet. Ignoring a cat when he's noisy sends a strong message that howling won't get him what he wants.

Stress or grieving

Some cats howl due to anxiety caused by major changes, such as moving house or adding a new person or pet to the household. The loss of a person or animal the cat loved may also cause howling due to grief. In either case, provide plenty of positive attention and try to keep other aspects of the cat's life as consistent as possible by maintaining the usual routines and not imposing additional changes. Many owners find that using a cat pheromone product such as Feliway has a calming effect.

Boredom and restlessness

Indoor cats can grow bored and restless without sufficient opportunities to exercise, and a formerly outdoor cat that has been confined to the house may be especially frustrated. To reduce howling caused by boredom, restlessness, or the desire to be outdoors:

- Have pets spayed or neutered to eliminate the biological urge to roam (this will also prevent yowling as a mate-seeking behaviour).
- Engage in regular play sessions that enable the cat to practice his hunting behaviours – tiring him out with play in the daytime is particularly useful for a cat that tends to be noisy at night.
- Leave solo toys such as catnip mice lying around for him to play with on his own.
- Harness train the cat and take him for walks.

- Provide some entertainment, such as a fish tank or a screened window with a view of a bird feeder.
- Grow some cat grass and catnip indoors.
- Hide treats around the house so that the cat can engage in a scavenger hunt that satisfies his natural hunting urges.
- If the cat is alone for long periods of time in the day or night, consider having a friend or relative pop by to provide some attention, as he may be howling out of loneliness as well as boredom.

Queen B demands attention, Jennifer Copley

Feline cognitive dysfunction syndrome

Like people, cats can suffer a cognitive decline as they get older, and some develop a condition called cognitive dysfunction syndrome (CDS). Also known as feline dementia, CDS can impair a cat's sleep cycle, which increases the likelihood of night-time vocalization and restlessness.

A cat with CDS may howl because he feels confused and anxious or because he's looking for others in the household and can't find them. Loss of hearing or vision in older cats may also contribute to howling.

Many older cats suffer from other medical conditions, so a full check-up is required to rule out illness before assuming the problem is dementia. A veterinarian may prescribe medication in the case of severe anxiety.

If other medical problems have been ruled out, options for calming the CDS sufferer's anxieties include spending more quality time with him during the day, using a pheromone product such as Feliway, and hiding treats or catnip toys around the house to provide pleasant distractions at night.

Vocal cat breeds

Siamese cats (and many breeds derived from the Siamese) tend to be more talkative by nature. In the case of naturally chatty breeds, if there have been no changes in vocalization (loudness, frequency, etc.), chattiness is unlikely to indicate a problem.

References

- ASPCA Virtual Pet Behaviorist. (2009). "Meowing and Yowling," "Behavior Problems in Older Cats," and "Enriching Your Cat's Life." ASPCABehavior.org.
- Sacramento SPCA. (2008). "Your Talkative Cat." SSPCA.org.
- Sueda, K., DVM., Best Friends Animal Society. (n.d.). "The Talkative Cat." BestFriends.org.

Chapter 5: Social Behaviours

Foster kittens meeting for the first time, Jennifer Copley

Do cats prefer to be alone?

Catisse and Catson, Jennifer Copley

Cats are actually very sociable, and most prefer to have company, though they can be fussy about who they spend time with (much like people).

Cats that have been properly socialized enjoy spending time with people, whereas cats that are aloof and unaffectionate have usually been abused or neglected during the critical period for socialization (between 3 and 16 weeks of age).

Although cats are more sociable than most people believe, you shouldn't put two adult cats together and assume that they'll get along. Introductions between adult cats need to be handled slowly and carefully. Kittens, on the other hand, aren't so fussy about their companions, and it's better to adopt two kittens rather than one so they can keep each other company.

Feline social groups

Feral cats form groups around available food sources and go off to hunt and scavenge on their own only when food is scarce. Feline colony sizes are quite variable, ranging from 2-15 individuals.

Related females and their young form the core of a feral cat colony, and one or more older males are usually attached to the group as well, though they may also mate with females from other groups. Some tomcats stay relatively close to a single colony, whereas others have wide-ranging territories.

Resident cat Freya hangs out with a trio of foster kittens: Calista, Nova, and Leo, Jennifer Copley

The overall size of a feral cat group is determined by the availability of food sources and resting and hiding places, with some areas supporting bigger colonies than others. When cats must rely solely on hunting for their food, groups tend to be smaller, but where there are scavenging opportunities (such as a nearby garbage dump), larger feline colonies are found.

Resident cat Smokey grooms an older foster kitten named The Earl of Grey, Jennifer Copley

Cooperative rearing of kittens

In feral cat colonies, females usually act as midwives during the birth of one another's kittens and cooperatively raise their young, nursing, nesting, guarding, and grooming communally as well as teaching kittens how to behave appropriately among other cats.

Female cats in a colony will often band together to repel other animals, including lone cats and cats from other colonies that encroach on their territory. They may eventually allow a stranger to join after a number of interactions, but unknown cats can't just walk into a territory and expect to be accepted.

In addition to protecting against invading tomcats, feral males have been observed caring for kittens in their own colonies. Some males share their food with young cats, groom them, and curl up around those that have been abandoned to keep them warm. Some even break up fights between kittens, separating them gently with a paw when a fight gets out of hand.

A lapful of foster kittens, Jennifer Copley

Group bonding and friendships

Within any given cat group, there are usually subgroups of 2 or more cats that spend a lot of time grooming each other and maintaining physical contact. Such friendships may occur between females, males, or a female and a male. Cats are more likely to become best friends with relatives such as siblings, but close friendships can form among nonrelated individuals as well.

Picatso and Catisse, Jennifer Copley

Feline hierarchy and conflict

While there are dominant and subordinate individuals in a cat colony, unlike dogs, cats don't maintain a clearly defined hierarchy wherein each individual is ranked above or below every other. There is often an alpha cat (usually the oldest female) who enjoys the highest status and privileged access to resources. Other cats usually decide who owns everything else on a case-by-case basis, and in some cases ownership of prime sleeping spots and other resources changes daily.

In-group fights are more likely when resources are scarce, both among feral and domestic cats. People who wish to introduce a new cat to a household with resident cats should keep this in mind, providing plenty of food bowls and litter boxes to reduce the likelihood of territorial conflicts.

When resources are plentiful, females in a group rarely fight. Males, on the other hand, will often fight for access to females, but the territories of tomcats tend to overlap, and no single male is able to monopolize all the females in his territorial range, no matter how good his fighting skills are.

Siblings playfighting, Jennifer Copley

Heavier males tend to rank more highly than their lighter counterparts when it comes to female mating preference within their own colonies. However, when they attempt to win females from other groups, they are sometimes defeated in fights with lighter males who belong to those groups, and females may show a preference for males from their own group regardless of size. This suggests that tomcats have a "home court advantage" when it comes to winning mates.

Kittens from the same litter are more likely to become best friends, Jennifer Copley

The sibling bond, Jennifer Copley

References:

- Aspinall, Victoria. (2006). *Complete Textbook of Veterinary Nursing*. Oxford, UK: Butterworth-Heinemann.
- Crowell-Davis, S. (1 November 2006). "CVC Highlights: Dispelling the Myth of the Asocial Cat." VeterinaryMedicine.dvm360.com.
- Dards, J.L. (1976). "Feral Cat Behaviour and Ecology." *Bulletin of the Feline Advisory Bureau, 15*(3). FeralCats.org.uk.
- Jongman, E.C., & Werribee, V. (2007). "Does Confinement Improve the Welfare of Domestic Cats?" RSPCA.org.au.
- Shojai, A.D. (2005). *PETiQuette: Solving Behavior Problems in Your Multi-Pet Household*. New York: M. Evans and Company, Inc.
- Yamane, A.; Doi, T.; & Ono, Y. (1996). "Mating Behaviors, Courtship Rank and Mating Success of Male Feral Cat (Felis catus)." *Journal of Ethology, 14*(1), pp. 35-44.

How can I encourage my new cat and my resident cat to bond?

Resident cat Smokey with newly adopted Sage, Jennifer Copley

Throwing animals together and hoping they'll get along can have disastrous consequences. Introducing cats the right way helps to promote harmony in a multi-cat home.

If you already have one or more cats, bringing home a new cat can be a traumatic experience for them – and for the new arrival. Cats find change extremely stressful, and their reactions are unpredictable. By handling the introduction properly, you can increase the likelihood of domestic harmony.

Resident cat Freya washes three foster kittens, Jennifer Copley

Bringing a new cat home

Start the new cat off in her own room for at least one day and preferably longer – some cats may require more than a week of separation, depending on prior experience. A cat that has lived with other cats in the past will probably adjust more quickly than a cat that has always lived alone.

Ideally, your resident cat should have access to your bedroom. The new cat should have her own food and water bowls, toys, litter box, and perch in her own area of the house or apartment. Your resident cat and the newcomer will be able to smell one another on your hands as you go from room to room, which will help them become familiar and comfortable with one another's scents.

Feed the two cats or give them treats on either side of the door that separates them so they can eat together without the anxiety of a visual confrontation. This creates a positive association by linking the other cat's scent with the enjoyment of food. During this transition, spend lots of quality time with each cat to soothe their anxieties.

21-year-old resident cat Laya with 8-week-old foster kitten Leo, Jennifer Copley

First interactions

Once the cats appear to be comfortable with one another on either side of the door, you can try opening the door a crack so that they can see one another but not actually walk through the door. Some hissing is normal, but if either of the cats becomes violent, close the door immediately and leave them alone in their respective territories for awhile before trying again.

If the cats take to one another and show no signs of agitation, the door can be opened permanently. However, if they're still not comfortable with each other, you can gradually increase the time you hold the door slightly open until they show no signs of aggression. Even if the cats are interacting without hostility, the door to the new cat's territory should be kept open so that she can escape if she feels threatened. Maintain separate food bowls (a comfortable distance apart), as well as a litter box for each cat.

Resident cat Freya with The Earl of Grey, Jennifer Copley

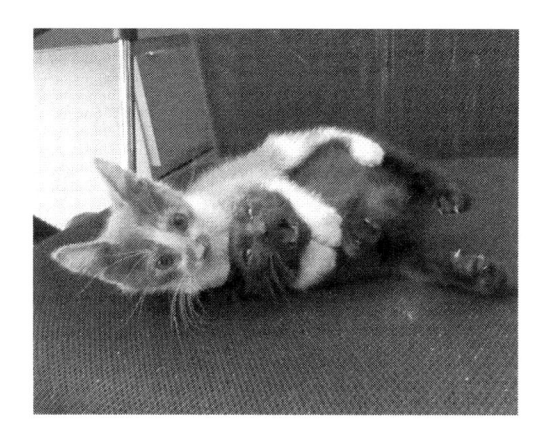

Playfighting foster kittens, Jennifer Copley

Worst-case scenario

What if the two cats never make peace with one another? Cats will become friends or at least coexist peacefully in most cases. However, in a worst-case scenario they will fight tooth and nail every time they see one another, in which case there are several options. You could alternate free roaming privileges, having one cat confined for part of each day so the other has a run of most of the rooms. Alternatively, assuming you have sufficient space, you could allow each cat to claim half of the house and keep a door closed or put up a barrier to keep them from venturing into one another's territory. The third option is to find another home for the newer cat.

References

- Ohio State University College of Veterinary Medicine: "Introducing New Pets." IndoorPet.OSU.edu.
- Feinman, J., VMD, CVH. "Introducing New Pets to Resident Pets." HomeVet.com.

Why do cats rub against things?

Sage rubs his face on the corner of a table, Jennifer Copley

Scent marking is a form of communication. Cats have scent glands in various places on their bodies, including their feet, flanks, and faces, through which they can release pheromones (chemical messages). By engaging in different types of rubbing, cats mark their territory and establish group scents, which help to maintain group identity in multi-cat households. When cats rub up against one another, the activity is called allorubbing.

Full-body contact

A cat will often rub his entire body along his favourite humans to mark them as part of his group. Scent can also be transferred when an owner strokes a cat. Some cats will hiss at a well-known human who has recently stroked a cat that is not part of the home group because they feel threatened by the other cat's scent.

Chinning

Cats often rub the sides of their faces on things, an activity called "chinning." They do this because they have scent glands on their chins and lips, which they use to override the scents left by other animals. Often, when a cat encounters a residual scent left by another animal, he will engage in a prolonged episode of chinning until he's sure that he has claimed the spot for himself.

Head-butting

Head-butting (also known as bunting), is an affectionate gesture. Cats will head-butt only those they feel affectionate toward and trust completely. Head butting often precedes full body rubbing, and cats will usually only do this when they're in a good mood.

The Earl of Grey affectionately head-butts Smokey, Jennifer Copley

References

- Nash, H., DVM, MS. (2008). "Why Do Cats Rub Against Legs and Furniture?" PetEducation.com.
- Tabor, R. (1997). *Understanding Cat Behaviour*. Cincinnati, OH: F&W Publications, Inc.

Why do cats roll on their backs to greet people?

Sage invites a belly rub, Jennifer Copley

When a cat shows you his belly, it's usually a sign of trust because he's putting himself in a vulnerable position. A cat that rolls on his back and presents his tummy is saying you're a friend, and that your relationship is cooperative rather than competitive. However, some cats will also roll on their backs when they want to play, as it gets them into a good position to tackle a proffered hand, so it's risky to assume that this gesture is always an invitation to a belly scratch, particularly with an unknown cat.

A cat may have mixed feelings, wanting to trust but feeling wary, particularly if he was handled roughly in the past. He might invite a tummy rub, but then become fearful and launch a warning attack on your hand. Such attacks are not usually done at full strength. They're a way of letting you know that the cat wants to trust but has been mistreated in the past and is prepared to defend himself if you take advantage of his vulnerability.

Kittens that were taken away from their mothers too early and not properly socialized are more likely to behave ambivalently, switching from friendly tummy display to attack mode. Poorly socialized cats also don't understand the appropriate level of force to use when playing, so their attacks may be more forceful than the typical warning swat or grab and release.

Some cats enjoy a brief tummy rub but soon warn the person off because petting becomes irritating due to static electricity. Cats may also attack when their bellies are petted because they have injuries or other medical problems that cause pain.

Reference: Tabor, R. (2005). *100 Ways to Understand Your Cat*. Cincinnati, OH: David & Charles.

A playful foster kitten, Jennifer Copley

Chapter 6: Strange Attractions

Smokey stops to smell a rose, Jennifer Copley

Why do some cats suck on fabric, wool, or hair?

A young foster kitten poses for a photo, Jennifer Copley

Many cats develop a habit of chewing on wool, fabric, or hair (or, less commonly, other materials such as cardboard or plastic). This self-comforting obsessive-compulsive behaviour is similar to thumb-sucking in human children.

Chewing or sucking fabric or wool is particularly common in cats that were weaned too early. Early weaning may also cause cats to suck on an owner's earlobes or fingers or attempt to suckle on other pets. Cats should never be taken from their mothers before 8 weeks of age, and ideally should stay with them for at least 12.

Wool or fabric sucking may also be triggered by stressful life events such as the death of a loved one, harassment by another pet, or moving house. In many cases, the behaviour diminishes as the cat grows older, though some cats retain it throughout their lives.

Certain breeds, such as the Siamese and Burmese, are more inclined to develop the habit, which indicates that genetics contribute to the likelihood of engaging in this behaviour. These breeds need to nurse for longer, so they are more likely develop neurotic habits with early weaning.

How to stop cats from sucking on wool or fabric

The habit is usually harmless unless the cat is actually swallowing pieces of fabric or knitted items (balls of wool should never be given to cats, as the wool can get caught on the barbs of their tongues, forcing them to swallow over and over again). Many owners tolerate this behaviour if the targeted items aren't actually being ruined.

If you want to stop your cat from sucking or chewing on wool or fabric and it's not convenient to keep targeted objects out of reach, there are safe spray-on cat deterrents such as Grannick's Bitter Apple® and Veterinarian's Best® Bitter Cherry Spray. If the behaviour is triggered by a stressful life event, providing additional reassurance and attention can be beneficial. Giving the cat something similar to the targeted item that he's allowed to chew can also help.

Don't give the cat any attention, positive or negative, when he chews or suckles on inappropriate items, as this will reinforce the behaviour. Making a fuss or punishing the cat is unlikely to reduce the behaviour and may actually increase it.

Foster kittens that lost their mother too early attempt to nurse from a sibling, Jennifer Copley

How to stop cats from chewing on hair

If your hair is the target, putting it up under a cap can help to break the habit.

Some cases of hair chewing are caused by a love of hair products (many of which contain oils or other fats that taste delicious to pets) rather than stress or early weaning. If your cat is attracted to your hair products because he likes their flavour, switching to a less tasty conditioner or gel should solve the problem.

If your cat is interested in your hair only when you have been in a pool recently, it's the chlorine that's attracting his attention (chlorine smells like feline pheromones to some cats). Washing your hair directly after swimming will prevent hair chewing by chlorine-loving cats.

Many of our orphaned foster kittens attempt to nurse from blankets, particularly this furry blanket, Jennifer Copley

References

- Hillestad, K., DVM., Drs. Foster & Smith Veterinary & Aquatic Services Department. (2010). "Fabric Eating (Wool Sucking) in Cats." PetEducation.com.
- Pukey, B., DVM. (5 May 2008). "Nothing Odd About Cat Chewing Fabric." Canada.com.

Why do cats go crazy for catnip, mint, and valerian?

Catnip flowering, Jennifer Copley

Nepeta Cataria, commonly known as catnip, is appealing to cats because it contains nepetalactone, a volatile oil that mimics feline pheromones. These pheromones trigger a response in the hypothalamus and amygdala, brain structures that play a critical role in the regulation of emotions and responses to stimuli, and mediate appetite and sexual and predatory behaviours. The result is excitement, euphoria, predatory playfulness, and/or sexual behaviour, depending on the cat.

Because catnip is a member of the mint family, some cats are also attracted to mint plants. Catnip and fresh mint leaves aren't harmful to cats, though certain essential oils, including peppermint oil, are toxic to them.

Valerian, another cat-attractant and intoxicant, has a stimulating effect due to a substance called actinidine, which induces similar reactions to nepetalactone. Cats get excited and sometimes even a little aggressive under its influence. Fresh-growing valerian isn't harmful to cats, though some highly concentrated medications containing it may not be safe for them.

Catnip responses

The effects of catnip vary from one cat to the next. Common behavioural responses include:

- Chasing/stalking
- Chewing or batting at the catnip
- Feistiness
- Increased playfulness
- Kicking with the back feet
- Reduced inhibitions
- Rolling around on the floor
- Rubbing their heads or bodies in the herb
- Salivation
- Strange vocalizations

Nimbus playing with a catnip toy, Jennifer Copley

Post-catnip relaxation, Jennifer Copley

Catnip's effects last for approximately 10 minutes, followed by a period of about 30 minutes during which the cat is immune to it.

Cats can't become addicted to catnip, though they may stop responding to it with frequent exposure.

Catnip has no adverse health consequences for cats regardless of how often they indulge. It makes them happy and has the added benefit of diverting them from snacking on houseplants.

Cats need to snack on greenery from time to time, and while indoor cats are safer and live longer, on average, the indoor lifestyle deprives them of natural fresh-growing grass. Catnip is easy to grow, so owners may wish to create a little cat garden in a low pot or tray, with catnip and cat grass (barley, rye, or oats) to provide indoor cats with some greens.

Many cats just sniff or roll in catnip, but some like to eat it. Eating a lot of catnip can make a cat throw up. If your cat tends to gobble fresh or dried catnip and then vomit, switch to catnip toys.

Pablo strikes a pose, Jennifer Copley

The catnip response is hereditary. Approximately 70% of cats are natural responders (responder estimates vary widely from one cat expert to the next). Male cats are more likely to be responders than females, and unneutered males tend to respond more strongly than neutered males, probably because nepetalactone resembles a chemical found in female cat urine.

Cats that are genetic catnip responders may not respond to the herb when under stress or in a new environment.

The benefits of catnip

Catnip can provide a number of benefits:

- Feuding cats (assuming they're catnip responders) may develop positive associations with one another if catnip is applied to the fur of one or both.
- Catnip may provide pain reduction for ill or injured cats.
- Catnip reduces inhibitions, which can help nervous, timid cats grow bolder and friendlier.
- Catnip makes cat toys more appealing and promotes energetic play, which is beneficial for helping obese cats lose weight.
- Catnip can be used during play to help stressed out cats relax.

References

- Dodman, N., Dr. (n.d.). "Catnip...and How It Affects Your Cat's Behavior." PetPlace.com.
- Veterinary & Aquatic Services Department, Drs. Foster & Smith. (2010). "Catnip and the Response in Cats." PetEducation.com.
- ASPCA. (2010). "Peppermint Oil." ASPCA.org.
- Feline Advisory Bureau. (n.d.). "The Cat Friendly Home." FABCats.org.
- Hartwell, S. (2008). "Catnip, Valerian, Honeysuckle and Other Cat-Attractant Plants." MessyBeast.com.
- Hodgkins, E.M., DVM. (2007). *Your Cat: Simple New Secrets to a Longer, Stronger Life.* New York, NY: Thomas Dunne Books.
- ScienceDaily.com. (28 August 2001). "Catnip Repels Mosquitoes More Effectively Than DEET."
- Turner, R., DVM. (29 May 2007). "How Does Catnip Work Its Magic on Cats?" ScientificAmerican.com.

Casper and Cadence, Jennifer Copley

Why do some cats like shoes, socks, or feet?

The Shoe Guardian, Lisa Zins, Flickr, Creative Commons 2.0

Some cats love to chew, suck, or rub their faces all over shoes, socks, or feet. Chewing on shoes or socks may be a variant of the fabric sucking behaviour often seen in cats that have been weaned too early. However, many cats just find the smell of shoes, dirty socks, and feet appealing. Various theories have been proposed to explain the feline foot obsession:

- A beloved owner's scent is highly concentrated on his feet, and by extension, his shoes and socks, and this scent has a comforting effect on the cat.

- Cats may like the taste of salt in sweaty footwear.

- Shoes and bare feet capture scents from the ground they walk over, so owners bring home a variety of interesting smells that tell the cat where they've been and what they've encountered along the way.

- Cats have scent glands in their cheeks, and they rub their faces on shoes and socks to cover scents that have been acquired during outdoor excursions, thereby re-staking their claim to these objects.

- Cats react to human pheromones in sweat the same way they react to catnip (which has an ingredient that mimics feline pheromones).

It's likely that several of these factors play a role, though pheromones may be a particularly strong draw, especially for cats that behave as though they have consumed catnip in the presence of shoes, socks, or feet.

According to Kohl et al. (2001), although pheromones are primarily associated with the apocrine glands found on areas of the body such as the armpits and genitals, the mouth and feet are also sites of pheromone production.

Reference: Kohl, J.V.; Atzmueller, M.; Fink, B.; & Grammer, K. (2001). "Integrating Neuroendocrinology and Ethology." *Neuroendocrinology Letters, 22*(5). NEL.edu.

Why do cats love boxes?

Rey hiding in a box on her first day with us, Jennifer Copley

Enclosed spaces provide a number of benefits for cats including safety, comfort, and opportunities to surprise prey from a hidden location, which all may contribute to the feline affinity for enclosed spaces.

Physical safety

An enclosed space provides protection from predators such as coyotes because cats that hide are less likely to be seen and more difficult to attack if they are spotted. Having places to hide would have been critical to the survival of wild cats, the ancestors of our modern house cats, and domestic felines have retained the instinct to keep themselves safe by seeking hiding spots.

Cats often retreat to enclosed spaces when they are in conflict with other household pets or people, especially if they fear physical attack. However, they may also retreat when they are angry at others because it gives them an opportunity to calm down and avoid picking a fight.

Psychological safety

Those who foster feral cats and kittens for animal rescue organizations know that providing boxes or kitty condos can significantly reduce the anxiety of terrified new arrivals because boxes make cats feel safe in unfamiliar places. They can observe their new environments through holes in their hiding spots and emerge when they feel confident that no one will attack them, so boxes give them a feeling of control in frightening situations. Many of the rescue cats we foster view us differently after we provide a box, possibly because they understand that a predator would not offer a sanctuary.

Our observations accord with the findings of a quarantine cattery study by Vinke et al. (2014). Stress was measured using the Kessler and Turner Cat-Stress-Score assessment scale, which incorporates behaviours, body postures, and mood indicators such as pupil dilation and ear and whisker positions. Cameras were used rather than having people continuously monitoring the cats to prevent human observer effects. The researchers found that cats with boxes showed less stress, and that cats without boxes attempted to hide behind whatever was available, such as their litter trays, indicating their desperate psychological need for hiding spaces.

Comfort

Many cats also love containers that are too small or open to be good hiding spaces. They squeeze themselves into little open-top boxes, sinks, flowerpots, bowls, cooking pots, and anything else that will accommodate them (the 'if-I-fits-I-sits' principle). This is probably a heat-seeking behaviour, as cats are more comfortable in warm environments where they can relax and don't have to expend metabolic energy keeping their bodies warm. Curling up in small containers helps them maintain a higher body temperature with no effort.

It's also possible that tight containers feel comforting, like a hug. Being squeezed into a small warm space may evoke the comfort and safety of early kittenhood when they spent their days squeezed in cozily among littermates and against their mothers' bodies. A box may be particularly comforting if it has an appealing scent (for example, a beloved human companion's unwashed clothing or catnip).

The comforting effects of small enclosures may explain why cats gravitate to tape squares on the floor, an amusing phenomenon that has been well-documented on the internet. Many people have found that if they stick duct tape to the floor to make squares, their cats will come over and sit in them, likely because the outlines are perceived as symbolic boxes, with the imaginary enclosures providing psychological benefits such as stress reduction.

If I fits, I sits; Smokey relaxes in a Tupperware container where he can watch me work, Jennifer Copley

Hunting

Unlike animals that hunt in packs, cats are solitary predators because they usually catch prey only large enough to feed one. Because they receive no help in chasing down and subduing their prey, they often ambush rodents or birds from hiding spots, which increases the likelihood of obtaining a meal while reducing the risk of being injured by a prey animal.

References

- Dodman, N. (2017). "Why cats love to sit on squares." PBS News Hour, PBS.org.
- Gardiner, B. (2015). "Why do cats love boxes so much?" *Wired,* Wired.com.
- Vinke, C. M.; Godijn, L. M.; & Van der Leij, W. J. R. (2014). "Will a hiding box provide stress reduction for shelter cats?" *Applied Animal Behaviour Science, 160*, pp. 86-93.

Why do some cats love bleach or chlorine?

Some cats react to chlorine as if it were catnip. They chew on an owner's hair or towel after he's been to the pool or try to lick surfaces that have been recently cleaned with bleach or cleaning products that contain it. Nobody knows for sure why some cats love bleach, but the most likely reason for this attraction is that the smell of chlorine is perceived as similar to certain constituents in cat urine.

Catnip and valerian exert their effects by mimicking cat sex pheromones, and chlorine may produce a similar effect in some cats. However, unlike catnip and valerian, which are safe for cats, chlorine is toxic, so they should be prevented from consuming it. If your cat has a chlorine obsession, shower well with soap after swimming, put your swimsuit and towel somewhere inaccessible until they can be washed, and close the doors to any room where you're using bleach to clean surfaces.

Because some cats may perceive bleach or ammonia (also found in many household cleaning products) as the urine of other cats, cleaning areas cats have sprayed or urinated with chlorine- or ammonia-based cleaners can backfire, causing the cat to keep targeting the same spot.

Cat urine should be cleaned with an enzymatic cleaner such as Nature's Miracle to remove all scent traces. Otherwise, the cat may believe that another cat has urinated there, which will compel him to re-stake his claim to the spot by spraying or urinating over the scent mark of his imaginary rival.

Reference: Cornell University College of Veterinary Medicine. (15 November 2006). "Feline Behavior Problems: House Soiling." Vet.Cornell.edu.

Chapter 7: Eating and Drinking

Freya, Smokey, Kaya, Sprocket, and Kismet having lunch, Jennifer Copley

Why do cats eat grass or houseplants?

A cat relaxes on a grassy lawn, Jennifer Copley

Wild hunting cats consume some greenery when they eat the stomach contents of their prey, and non-hunting pets may need to get this vegetable matter by other means, so grass eating is a natural behaviour. Even big cats such as cougars eat grass.

It's not known for sure why cats eat grass and other plants, but the most plausible theories are that grass is needed as:

- Roughage (for its laxative effects)
- An emetic (to help with vomiting up indigestible matter)
- A vitamin supplement

It's possible that all three of these requirements contribute to grass eating.

When cats consume prey whole in the wild, they often consume bones, fur, feathers, and other indigestible parts. Cats also swallow their own fur during grooming, and if hairballs form, they must be either vomited up or moved down through the digestive tract efficiently so they don't cause a digestive obstruction. Grass may help with inducing vomiting and providing laxative fiber that moves hairballs and other indigestible matter through the digestive system, preventing obstruction and constipation.

Some biologists have suggested that cats also eat grass to obtain small amounts of critical nutrients, particularly folic acid. Folic acid is a vitamin that aids in hemoglobin production and other functions, and animals that don't get enough folic acid from their diets can become anemic. Cats may eat grass to obtain trace amounts of this vitamin, and perhaps other nutrients as well.

Most cats will snack on grass if given the opportunity, and grass-eating is only a problem if the grass is coated in toxic pesticides. Ideally, indoor cats should be provided with a pot of cat grass (typically oat, wheat, barley, or rye grass) to consume as needed.

References

- Bush, B. (1984). *The Cat Care Question and Answer Book*. Boston, NY: Bookthrift Co.
- Busch, R. (2004). *The Cougar Almanac*. The Lyons Press.
- PetMD.com. (2010). "Why Do Cats Eat Grass?"
- Tobiassen Crosby, J., DVM. (n.d.). "Frequently Asked Question: Why Does My Dog (or Cat) Eat Grass?" About.com.

A friendly cat rolls in the grass, Jennifer Copley

Why do some cats eat kitty litter?

Foster kittens enduring a photography session, Jennifer Copley

Kitty litter eating is a common problem among kittens during the weaning process because young kittens may test various substances to determine whether or not they qualify as food. For this reason, clumping litter should never be used with kittens, and litter should be cleaned soon after it has been soiled.

If you catch your kitten eating litter, pick her up and remove the litter from her mouth immediately. Curious kittens (and in some cases, adult cats) may also swallow coins, paperclips, sewing needles, and other objects they find lying around, so it's important to put small objects away when not in use.

Although most adult cats don't eat litter, there is a condition called pica that can cause them to eat inappropriate things. Pica may result from:

- Nutritional deficiency
- Medical problems (such as neurological disorders or pancreatitis)
- Stress over household changes (such as the introduction of a new pet)
- Obsessive-compulsive disorder
- Boredom

Cats afflicted with pica may eat things that will poison them, damage their teeth, or obstruct their digestive tracts, leading to life-threatening complications, so a veterinarian should be consulted if a cat shows signs of this disorder.

If the cat is sucking or chewing on wool or fabric but not actually consuming the material, the problem isn't pica. Suckling behaviours in adult cats usually indicate that they were weaned too early or are suffering from stress.

References

- American Animal Hospital Association. (2010). "Pica: When Your Pet Eats Things That Aren't Food." HealthyPet.com.
- Bower, J., & Bower, C. (1998). *The Cat Owner's Problem Solver*. Pleasantville, NY: Reader's Digest Association, Inc./Andromeda Oxford Limited.
- Breyer, M. (4 October 2009). "Does Your Cat Eat Strange Things?" Care2.com.
- Fox, M. (1989). *The New Animal Doctor's Answer Book*. New York, NY: Newmarket Press.
- Plotnick, A., DVM. (26 July 2006). "Pica: When Cats Eat Weird Things." MahattanCats.com.
- Trott, K., & Snell, T., UC Davis School of Veterinary Medicine. (n.d.). "Unusual Eating Habits in Dogs and Cats." VetMed.UCDavis.edu.
- Van Lienden, R., DVM. (18 April 2006). "Cat Eating Cat Litter – Answered by Dr. Van Lienden." Pets.ca.

Why do some cats eat soap?

Rambler smiles for the camera, Jennifer Copley

Cats and dogs that eat soap are probably craving something they're not getting from their diets. Soaps (and many moisturizers and hair products) contain oils and other fats that pets find appealing.

An animal that regularly tries to eat soap or moisturizer may not be getting enough fat in his diet. If your pet is attracted to soaps or moisturizers, keep these products out of reach because many contain toxic substances and consult a veterinarian for dietary or supplement recommendations, or try switching to a higher-fat cat food.

Reference: Fox, M., Dr. (1989). *The New Animal Doctor's Answer Book*. New York, NY: Newmarket Press.

Why do some cats eat plastic?

Gizmo chews on a plastic replica of Starbug (which was removed after the photo was taken because there was a risk that he would swallow the ship's feet), Jennifer Copley

Tallow (rendered animal fat), petroleum products, and gelatin are used in the manufacturing of some plastics, and gelatin is also used in photograph emulsion. Cats that are drawn to plastics and photographs may be suffering from pica, which is caused by nutritional deficiency, stress, boredom, or medical problems.

Reference: Plotnick, A., DVM. (26 July 2006). "Pica: When Cats Eat Weird Things." MahattanCats.com.

How can I stop my cat from eating inappropriate items?

A foster kitten contemplates chewing on a plant, Jennifer Copley

If your cat is eating or licking cat litter, dirt, soap, or other inappropriate objects or substances:

- Consult a veterinarian to rule out medical problems and discuss diet and supplementation options.
- If litter eating is the problem, change the type of litter in case something about the brand is causing the cat to perceive it as food.
- Keep targeted objects out of reach whenever possible or spray them with safe deterrents such as Grannick's Bitter Apple® or Veterinarian's Best® Bitter Cherry Spray.
- If the problem is psychological, try to eliminate or reduce the stressor and provide extra attention.
- Rather than a couple of large meals, feed the cat many small meals over the course of the day and provide a pot of cat grass to give her something healthy to chew between meals.
- Reduce boredom by providing plenty of solo play toys (for example, catnip mice, balls, etc.) as well as playtime with interactive toys (laser pointers, wand toys), things to climb (cat trees, wall-mounted climbing shelves or walks, etc.), healthy treats hidden around the house, and an interesting view (such as a birdfeeder outside a window).

References

- American Animal Hospital Association. (2010). "Pica: When Your Pet Eats Things That Aren't Food." HealthyPet.com.
- Bower, J., & Bower, C. (1998). *The Cat Owner's Problem Solver*. Pleasantville, NY: Reader's Digest Association, Inc./Andromeda Oxford Limited.
- Breyer, M. (4 October 2009). "Does Your Cat Eat Strange Things?" Care2.com.
- Fox, M. (1989). *The New Animal Doctor's Answer Book*. New York, NY: Newmarket Press.
- Plotnick, A., DVM. (26 July 2006). "Pica: When Cats Eat Weird Things." MahattanCats.com.
- Trott, K., & Snell, T., UC Davis School of Veterinary Medicine. (n.d.). "Unusual Eating Habits in Dogs and Cats." VetMed.UCDavis.edu.
- Van Lienden, R., DVM. (18 April 2006). "Cat Eating Cat Litter – Answered by Dr. Van Lienden." Pets.ca.

Helix captures artificial prey, Jennifer Copley

Why do some cats drink from the toilet when they have fresh tap water available?

Curious Lynx peers into a glass, Jennifer Copley

Cats often perplex their owners by ignoring a freshly filled bowl of water and instead choosing to drink from muddy puddles, glasses of water that have been sitting around overnight, or even the toilet.

Cats have a far better sense of smell than people, which affects their sense of taste as well, and some cats find the chlorine in tap water unpleasant. Standing water in a toilet bowl or glass that has been left out overnight is free of chlorine because the chlorine dissipates over time, and rainwater in outdoor puddles is free of chlorine to begin with, so many cats prefer it.

Reference: Morris, D. (1987). *Catlore*. London, UK: Jonathan Cape Ltd.

Why has my cat stopped eating?

Resident cats Sage, Freya, and Smokey and 2 foster kittens share a plate of food, Jennifer Copley

Cats may stop eating due to problems with their food, problems with the food bowl or its location, obtaining food from other sources, or medical or dental problems.

Problems with the food

- *The food is stale*: Dry food can become stale, particularly in warm weather or when exposed to moisture. A bag or box of dry food may need to be replaced if the cat has suddenly gone off it.
- *The food is too cold*: Cats like their food warm, or at least at room temperature. If wet food has been in the refrigerator, it may be unappealing to your cat. If this is the problem, heat food to a lukewarm temperature before serving.
- *The food doesn't provide sufficient protein*: Many cat foods are made primarily of filler such as cornmeal or rice. Check the ingredients list on your cat's food to ensure that the first ingredient is meat, ideally high-quality protein rather than a by-product. Only feed your cat good quality commercial foods or natural diets recommended by your veterinarian.
- *The cat dislikes or has become bored with the brand or flavour of food*: If you have tried replacing stale dry food or warming wet food and your cat still refuses to eat, providing something new may rekindle his interest in food.

Problems with the food bowl or its location

- *There is an audience*: Most cats want privacy while they eat, so it's a good idea to keep the cat's bowls away from high-traffic areas of the house.
- *They're bothered by the presence of other pets*: If your cat seems anxious when eating with other household cats or dogs, try feeding pets in separate areas of the house, if possible.
- *The food bowl is dirty*: Cats will usually refuse fresh food from a bowl that has bits of old stale food clinging to it, as this can cause bacterial contamination.
- *They're allergic to their food bowls*: Some cats develop an allergy to plastic food bowls, which can cause tiny sores on their lips.
- *The bowl gives off electric shocks*: Some metal bowls give off small static electric shocks, particularly in cold, dry weather.

Other (nonmedical) reasons why cats refuse food

- *He has already eaten:* Outdoor cats may snack over the course of their travels, either catching small prey animals or eating food that neighbours put out for their own pets. Cats that receive table scraps regularly are also more likely to reject regular cat food.
- *He's manipulating you:* If you give your cat treats every time he refuses his regular cat food, he'll quickly learn that he can easily trick you by pretending to lose his appetite.

Medical and dental problems

A cat that refuses food due to stress or dislike of a particular cat food brand will eventually succumb to hunger if he's healthy. If your cat is still refusing food after 24 hours, you should bring him to a veterinarian as soon as possible to check for medical or dental problems. Other symptoms that indicate medical problems include:

- Persistent vomiting
- Lethargy
- Weight loss
- Dull coat/failure to groom
- Diarrhea
- Constipation
- Fever
- Urinating or defecating outside the litter box
- Change in vocalization (i.e., the cat starts howling regularly)

Symptoms of dental problems such as severe gingivitis or mouth abscess include:

- Very bad breath
- Swollen or red gums
- Allowing food to fall from the mouth

Consult a veterinarian if any of these additional symptoms are present.

References

- High Peaks Cat Shelter. (n.d.). "Refusing to Eat." HPCatShelter.org.
- Purina. (n.d.). "Fussy Eaters." Purina.co.uk.
- King County Animal Care and Control. (2007). "Finicky Eater." KingCounty.gov.

Hadron and Collider lost their appetites due to a rare, life-threatening illness; with syringe feeding and supplemental fluid injections, they made a full recovery, Jennifer Copley

Why do some cats suddenly develop voracious appetites?

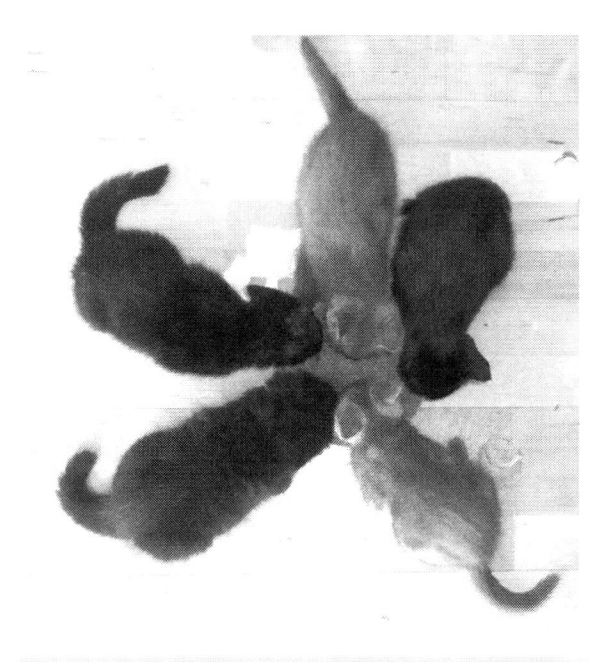

5 foster kittens eating together, Jennifer Copley

If a cat with a normal appetite suddenly becomes insatiable, this may indicate a medical problem. Excessive eating (polyphagia) often includes some of the following behaviours:

- Accepting less desirable food that would have been ignored in the past
- Jumping on kitchen counters to steal food
- Eating an entire meal in one session
- Eating rapidly enough to induce vomiting
- Pestering owners for extra feedings and snacks
- Begging or stealing food from neighbours

A visit to the veterinarian is required if the cat has any of the following illness symptoms in addition to increased appetite:

- Diarrhea
- Drinking more than usual
- Hyperactivity
- Increased vocalization (howling)
- Persistent vomiting
- Urinating more frequently
- Urinating or defecating outside the litter box
- Weight loss

Medical conditions that increase appetite in cats

Brain injury or disease

A trauma, tumour, or infection affecting the brain's satiety center can make it impossible for a cat to know when he's full and should stop eating. Treatment varies depending on the illness or injury.

Cancerous or benign tumours

Tumours that produce insulin, interfere with nutrient absorption, or cause the secretion of growth hormone may trigger an insatiable appetite. Treatments may include surgery, radiation, or chemotherapy.

Cushing's syndrome

Long-term use of corticosteroid medications and tumours of the adrenal and pituitary glands can cause the body to release excess cortisol, leading to hyperadrenocorticism (Cushing's syndrome). Symptoms include polyphagia, increased thirst and urination, and the development of a pot belly. Approximately 50% of adrenal tumours and the majority of pituitary tumours are benign. Treatment may involve weaning the cat off corticosteroids, surgically removing the afflicted gland, radiation, or medication.

Diabetes

The prevalence of diabetes among cats has skyrocketed due to cheap high-carbohydrate cat foods. In addition to polyphagia, symptoms of diabetes include increased thirst, increased urination, and weight loss or gain. Diabetes can be controlled with proper diet and insulin injections.

Hyperthyroidism

Hyperthyroidism speeds the body's metabolism, leading to hyperactivity, weight loss, intense hunger, and possibly diarrhea and vomiting. Treatment may involve medication, surgery, or radioactive iodine therapy.

Infections

Although microbial infections are more likely to cause loss of appetite, in some cases, particularly when the infection interferes with nutrient absorption, the cat may feel ravenous.

Inflammatory bowel disease (IBD) and irritable bowel syndrome (IBS)

IBD and IBS interfere with the absorption of nutrients, causing diarrhea, vomiting, weight loss (even if the cat eats large amounts of food), and in some cases, defecating outside the litter box. Treatments include medication and dietary changes.

Internal parasites

Parasitic infestations that can trigger increased appetite include tapeworms, roundworms, hookworms, and heartworms. Flea infestation and feeding raw meat increase the risk of internal parasites, as both can harbour worms. Prevention includes eradicating fleas, keeping cats indoors, and routine deworming, particularly for outdoor cats.

Lymphocytic cholangitis

This disease of the liver can cause weight loss despite a big appetite. Lymphocytic cholangitis is treated with medication.

Pancreatic disorders

Disorders of the pancreas can cause vomiting and diarrhea or the passing of bulky, foul-smelling stools because nutrients are not digested properly. Treatment may involve medication, dietary changes, and withholding oral food and fluids while rehydrating with intravenous fluids.

Medications

Benzodiazepines, antihistamines, and many other medications can stimulate appetite in cats.

Feral kittens often have parasites, which are easily treated with medication (this kitten required treatment due to a severe infestation), Jennifer Copley

Non-medical causes of increased appetite

Boredom

Although indoor cats are safer and live longer, many begin overeating out of boredom. Providing an enriched environment (toys, cat trees, scratch posts, a view of a birdfeeder through the window, etc.) can keep indoor cats active and happy.

Cold environment

Metabolism may be increased via heat generation. Cold temperatures can cause animals to burn more calories producing heat, which makes them hungrier.

Competition at the food bowl

Worry that his food will be stolen by other pets can cause a cat to gorge out of panic. This problem can be solved by feeding pets in separate rooms with closed doors.

Increased exercise

If an owner plays with her cat more often, purchases an exciting new toy or cat tree, or takes the cat out walking on a leash, the cat will burn more calories than usual. The arrival of a new pet the cat plays with or fights with can also increase calorie burning, as can moving to a new home with stairs.

A foster kitten plays on a cat tree, Jennifer Copley

Poor quality cat food

Cheap high-carbohydrate cat foods don't meet a cat's nutritional requirements, so he may eat large amounts yet feel starved all the time, even if he's becoming obese. This problem can be fixed by switching to a premium high-protein cat food.

Pregnancy/growth

Pregnant and nursing cats and kittens experiencing growth spurts have very high calorie requirements.

Foster kittens Sola and Raya during their rapid adolescent growth spurt, Jennifer Copley

Psychological trauma

Many cats engage in comfort eating when under stress. The loss of a beloved human or animal, moving house, the arrival of a new pet or baby, or any other major change may trigger overeating. Polyphagia that results from psychological distress or boredom can be treated by:

- Providing extra attention
- Playing with the cat more often
- Substituting catnip for high-calorie treats
- Feeding reasonable portions
- Refusing to give in to demands for extra food

To be on the safe side, consult a veterinarian if there is any unexplained change in your cat's eating habits to rule out medical issues before assuming the problem is psychological.

References

- Brum, D. (2010). "Polyphagia (Increased Food Consumption) in Cats." PetPlace.com.
- Ettinger, S.J. (2001). *Pocket Companion to Textbook of Veterinary Internal Medicine*. Philadelphia, PA: W.B. Saunders Company.

- Feline Advisory Bureau. (2008). "Feline Hyperadrenocorticism (Cushing's Syndrome)." FABCats.org.
- Houpt, K.A. (n.d.). "Polyphagia." VetConnect.com.au.
- Lappin, M.R. (2001). *Feline Internal Medicine Secrets*. Philadelphia, PA: Hanley & Belfus, Inc.
- Mackin, A., & Ward, H.G. (2008). "Feline Weight Loss." *Irish Veterinary Journal, 61*(1), 40-44.
- Nash, H., Drs. Foster & Smith. (2010). "Common Diseases of Senior Cats." PetEducation.com.
- PetMD.com. (2010). "Increased Appetite in Cats."
- Shaw, D.H., & Ihle, S.L. (2006). *Small Animal Internal Medicine*. Oxford, UK: Blackwell Publishing Ltd.
- Slatter, DH. (2003). *Textbook of Small Animal Surgery*. Philadelphia, PA: Elsevier Science
- Sparkes, A.H. (2003). "Feline Hepatic Disease – Where are We Now?" 28th World Congress of the World Small Animal Veterinary Association, Veterinary Information Network, VIN.com.

It's normal for young, active cats to eat a lot, particularly if they spend most of their waking hours practicing their fighting moves, Jennifer Copley

Why do some cats drink so much and pee so often?

A 22-year-old cat with kidney disease; she was diagnosed at 17 but had many additional good years with weekly fluid injections, Jennifer Copley

There are a number of illnesses that can trigger excessive thirst (polydipsia) and urination (polyuria) in cats. Cats with polydipsia may drink from the shower, toilet, tub, sink faucets, or plant trays. Their litter boxes require scooping more often due to increased urination and their water bowls have to be refilled more frequently than in the past. Of course, many healthy cats drink from faucets and toilets, and normal water consumption and urination vary from one cat to the next. It's changes in a cat's habits that usually indicate a problem.

Illnesses that cause excessive thirst and increased urination in cats

The illnesses that most often trigger frequent urination and increased thirst in cats are:

- Kidney disease (also known as chronic renal failure or CRF)
- Diabetes mellitus
- Thyroid disease (hyperthyroidism)

These diseases are common in older cats, and the latter two also cause increased appetite. Other illnesses that can cause polydipsia and polyuria (some of which are quite rare) include the following.

Electrolyte abnormalities

- Low blood potassium (hypokalemia), typically resulting from symptoms of underlying illness such as appetite loss, vomiting, or diarrhea
- High blood calcium (hypercalcemia), often due to a tumour, kidney disease, or other health problem

Endocrine (hormonal) disorders

- Acromegaly, a condition whereby too much growth hormone is released into the system, often caused by a benign pituitary tumour
- Central diabetes insipidus, which may be triggered by head trauma, pituitary gland tumour, or unknown causes
- Hyperadrenocorticism (Cushing's disease), usually caused by a benign pituitary tumour
- Hypoadrenocorticism (Addison's disease), which can have a variety of different causes, the most common of which is an autoimmune reaction (the body's immune system attacking its own tissues)
- High red blood cell count (polycythemia), a symptom of many different illnesses
- Kidney infection (pyelonephritis)
- Liver disease
- Renal glycosuria, a kidney disorder caused by a disease or congenital defect
- Uterine infection (pyometra)

Treatment for polydipsia and polyuria varies based on the underlying cause.

Other causes of increased urination and thirst

Non-illness-related polydipsia and polyuria triggers include:

- Administration of diuretics, salt, or certain medications
- Hot temperatures
- Increased exercise
- Post-obstructive diuresis (increased urination after removal of a urinary obstruction)
- Switching from wet food to dry (many cats on dry-food-only diets are chronically dehydrated, so they feel very thirsty)

Psychogenic polydipsia, a rare obsessive-compulsive behavioural problem, can also cause excessive fluid consumption. Treatments for this condition include behaviour modification therapy and gradual water restriction. In severe cases, a veterinarian may prescribe medication to reduce obsessive-compulsive behaviour.

Symptoms of illness that may accompany polydipsia and polyuria

Additional symptoms that indicate a medical problem include:

- Behavioural changes
- Constipation
- Diarrhea
- Having accidents outside the litter box
- Increased appetite
- Lethargy
- Loss of weight and/or appetite
- Poor coat condition
- Vomiting
- Weakness

If you notice a change in your cat's drinking or urination habits, consult a veterinarian.

References

- Bennett, P., BVSc, FACVSc, DipACVIM. (2003). "Polyuria and Polydipsia." Australian College of Veterinary Scientists – Science Week 2003 – Small Animal Medicine Chapter Meeting.

- Fenner, W.R., et al. (2000). *Quick Reference to Veterinary Medicine, Third Edition*. Baltimore, MD: Lippincott Williams & Wilkins.
- Lappin, M.R., DVM, PhD. (2001). *Feline Internal Medicine Secrets*. Philadelphia, PA: Hanley & Belfus Inc.
- Melin, E., DVM., Westgate Pet Clinic. (n.d.). "What is Polyuria/Polydipsia? AKA: Why is My Pet Drinking and Urinating so Much?" WagsandWhiskers.com.
- Osborne, C.A., DVM, PhD, DiplACVIM. (1 June 2003). "The Ins and Outs of Polyuria and Polydipsia." *DVM360*. VeterinaryNewsDVM360.com.
- PetMD.com. (n.d.). "Increased Thirst and Urination in Cats."
- Petplace Veterinarians. (2011). "Polydipsia and Polyuria (Excessive Drinking and Urinating) in Cats." PetPlace.com.

Chapter 8: Hunting

Helix "hunting", Jennifer Copley

Why do cats play with their prey?

Nimbus plays with his "prey," Jennifer Copley

There's a common misconception that cats torment their prey for fun, but cats have an instinct to play with their prey because it's the only way they can make a kill without risking injury.

Cats kill their prey by delivering a neck bite that severs the spinal cord. To do this, they must temporarily release their prey to get at the nape of its neck, so the prey animal may escape or counterattack.

Small animals will defend themselves if they get the chance. Mice, rats, and other rodents can deliver a vicious bite, and birds can peck. A cat has a very short muzzle; to get close enough to apply the neck bite, she risks injury to her eyes and face.

A cat will "play" with her prey to tire it out, reducing her risk of injury, but she's not actually playing in the human sense. She's simply doing the job that her instincts tell her she must do to avoid starvation and protect herself in the process. If the prey is lively, the cat could suffer a serious bite that might become infected, leading to her death. She can make the kill safely only when the prey is tired and dazed.

Sometimes a cat will appear to lose interest when the prey becomes still, but then leap upon it as soon as it moves. This gives the impression that the cat is toying with the poor creature, but it's just the cat's way of ensuring that the prey is sufficiently dazed to safely finish it off. If she attempts to finish things too quickly, she could risk failure or serious injury.

Although they know that hunting is a natural behaviour, most cat owners don't want to see other animals harmed. There are a number of ways to prevent cats from catching birds and small mammals, including putting bells on their collars and ensuring that bird feeders are out of reach. All cats have the hunting instinct, but in well-fed housecats this behaviour can be redirected toward toys designed to simulate prey.

Reference: Tabor, Roger. (1997). *Understanding Cat Behaviour*. Cincinnati, OH: F&W Publications, Inc.

Sage captures an artificial bird, Jennifer Copley

Why do cats make chattering sounds when they see birds through a window?

A chattering kitten, Jennifer Copley

Ethologist Desmond Morris describes the chattering sounds a cat makes when she sees a bird through a window as a "vacuum activity." Vacuum activities occur when the cat is unable to fulfill her natural hunting drive.

When a cat sees a bird or other prey animal she can't get to, she tenses her body and chatters her teeth as a substitute for delivering the killing neck bite. This action likely represents a combination of excitement at seeing an enticing prey animal and the frustration of having her hunting drive thwarted.

Frustration can be reduced by playing with your cat using toys that simulate prey (such as a fishing pole toy with a cloth mouse or feathers at the end of a string). Interactive wand play allows cats to practice their hunting skills without killing anything.

Reference: Morris, D. (1987). *Catlore*. London, UK: Jonathan Cape Ltd.

Why do cats bring home live prey?

Aspen plays with a toy mouse, Jennifer Copley

Many cats bring dead animals home as "gifts" for their loved ones, but some also bring in live prey to present to their owners, as they would for their kittens to let them practice their hunting skills. A cat that brings live prey to her owner may believe her human companion would appreciate the opportunity to practice these valuable skills.

Some cats bring live prey to an area of the home they consider their own space rather than presenting the animals to their owners. A cat that does this gives herself a home court advantage – if she needs to recapture the prey in its own territory, it will have a better chance of escaping, whereas on her own turf, she knows the layout and all the escape routes.

Reference: Tabor, R. (1997). *Understanding Cat Behaviour*. Cincinnati, OH: F&W Publications, Inc.

Chapter 9: Behaviour Problems

Max scratches a chair, Jennifer Copley

Why do some cats pull out their fur?

Sage is an occasional fur plucker, Jennifer Copley

Cats spend up to one-quarter of their waking lives grooming, and some biting or aggressive licking is normal. However, fur pullers take this further, using their teeth to remove chunks of fur, usually leaving bald patches or areas with short, stubby fur. In some cases, the exposed skin becomes red and irritated.

The most common causes of fur pulling are flea infestation, allergies, infections, and obsessive-compulsive disorder triggered by anxiety (otherwise known as psychogenic alopecia, or hair loss due to psychological issues). If you have taken your cat for a veterinary check-up to rule out other causes, the fur pulling is probably attributable to psychogenic alopecia, particularly if the cat shows other symptoms of stress such as behaving irritably or having accidents outside the litter box (though some cats pull out their fur with no other anxiety indicators).

Many cats become anxious as a result of major life changes such as moving house or the arrival of a new baby or another pet, or due to deprivation or abuse in their past (which can cause lifelong anxiety), though some are just genetically predisposed to be anxious.

Anxious cats often engage in repetitive actions such as fur pulling or excessive grooming to comfort themselves because these behaviours increase production of the body's natural opiates, which decrease stress.

Like fur pulling, excessive grooming or licking may be caused by parasites, allergies, infections, or stress. Some cats that pull out their fur also overgroom, licking a spot obsessively if it's itchy or painful or as a self-soothing behaviour in the case of anxiety.

Cats on low-fat diets may develop flaky, dry skin, and the subsequent irritation can lead to excessive grooming or fur pulling. In this case, changing to a higher-fat diet should fix the problem.

Treatments for psychogenic alopecia

A cat that is pulling out his fur or grooming obsessively should have a veterinary checkup to rule out illnesses, infections, allergies, dietary insufficiencies, and parasite infestation before treating the behaviour as a sign of psychological distress.

Psychogenic alopecia can usually be treated by making changes to your cat's environment:

- *Decrease stress:* Identify stressors in your cat's life and eliminate as many as possible.
- *Provide more attention:* Spend more time playing with and petting your cat to reduce her anxiety.
- *Provide places to hide:* If stress is caused by other household pets, provide plenty of perches, hiding tents, cardboard boxes, or cubbies so the cat has safe spaces where she can get away from other animals.
- *Elizabethan collars:* In cases of fur pulling or overgrooming to the point where sores develop on the targeted spots, your veterinarian may recommend using a cone-shaped medical collar for awhile to break the habit.

- *Medication:* In severe cases, your veterinarian may prescribe an anti-anxiety medication. However, this should be considered a last resort because these medications can have side effects and cats may become physically dependent on benzodiazepines.

If your cat is pulling out her fur, don't reward the behaviour. Providing attention in response to aggressive grooming may act as a reinforcement, ensuring that she continues to pull out her fur. Punishing the behaviour is also a bad idea, as punishment usually causes anxiety and an increase in problem behaviours rather than discouraging them.

Falcio washes a paw, Jennifer Copley

References

- Merck & Co., Inc., Eds. Cynthia M. Kahn, BA, MA & Scott Line, DVM, PhD, Dipl ACVB. (2007). *The Merck/Merial Manual for Pet Health, Home Edition.*
- Richards, M., DVM. (2007). "Behavior in Cats – Hair Damaging, Self Damaging." VetInfo4Cats.com.
- Schelling, C., Dr. (2005). "Psychogenic Alopecia." CatHealth.com.
- Whiteley, E., Dr. (2008). "How to Solve Cat Behaviour Problems." HowStuffWorks.com.

Why do cats have accidents outside the litter box (and how can they be prevented)?

Nova, a very clean kitten, had only one accident outside the box after meeting a dog, so the problem was likely attributable to either anxiety or territorial marking, Jennifer Copley

There's a popular misconception that cats urinate on their owners' beds or other inappropriate places as an act of revenge or spite, but urinating or defecating outside the litter box is actually caused by illness, anxiety, territorial conflicts, or problems with the litter box or litter.

The owner's bed (or clothing) is often chosen by an anxious or ill cat because it's a safe, soft place that has the comforting scent of a beloved human companion. The cat may also choose places where the urine is sure to be noticed because he's trying to communicate his distress about a psychological or physical problem.

A cat that has started peeing on the bed should be taken for a veterinary check-up to rule out urinary tract infections, kidney disease, hyperthyroidism, and other medical problems that can make urination urgent or painful. If the cat is given a clean bill of health, common non-medical causes of litter box avoidance include:

- *Dirty litter box:* Boxes should be scooped daily and washed weekly.
- *Chemical smells:* Use a mild detergent to clean the box and don't use perfumed litter.
- *Dislike of a covered box:* Remove the lid.
- *Too much or not enough litter:* Try different depths.
- *Preference for a softer surface:* Try a finer-grained litter.
- *Recently changed box location or litter:* Put things back the way they were and make changes gradually (move the box a few inches per day or mix the new litter in a little at a time with the old).
- *Bad litter box location:* Move the box to a quieter, low-traffic area of the home, away from food and water dishes.
- *Territorial competition:* Each cat should have his own box, and cats should be neutered or spayed to prevent territorial marking.
- *Other pets bother the cat while he uses the box:* Place the box somewhere where the cat is less likely to be harassed or doesn't feel cornered and can escape easily.
- *Mobility issues:* For elderly, very young, or mobility-challenged cats, switch to a box with lower sides, and make sure it's easily accessible (i.e., not up a flight of stairs).
- *Litter box is too small:* If the cat spends a lot of time scratching outside the box (floor, wall, etc.), he probably needs a bigger box; the box should be at least 1.5 times the length of the cat, not counting his tail.
- *Cat is scared by animals seen through a window:* If a window is at or near ground level, close the curtains to prevent the cat seeing other animals, as this can trigger territorial marking or fear-induced urination.
- *Cat has been declawed:* Digging in kitty litter is excruciatingly painful for newly declawed cats, and anxiety over the surgery may cause the cat to seek a comforting place to eliminate (declawing significantly increases the likelihood of litter box issues and other long-term behavioural problems).
- *Stressful changes such as moving house, a new baby or pet, a restricted diet, less attention from a favourite person, or the death of a beloved person or animal:* Provide extra attention and spend time playing with the cat; in extreme cases, anti-anxiety medication may be prescribed by a veterinarian.

Don't hit the cat, yell at him, or rub his nose in the urine. He won't associate the punishment with the act, so it will just increase his anxiety and make the problem worse.

How to stop a cat from urinating in inappropriate places

In addition to fixing the problem that triggered the behaviour, the targeted spot must be cleaned thoroughly, not just with regular washing products, but also with an enzymatic cleaner such as Nature's Miracle or The Equalizer that removes all traces. Otherwise the scent will keep luring the cat back to do it again.

If it's too inconvenient to keep the door to the targeted room closed, it may be necessary to use a deterrent until the habit is broken. Safe cat deterrents that can be placed on the targeted spot include:

- Plastic carpet runner, pointy side up
- Sticky Paws tape
- Motion-sensing devices that emit a burst of startling air when the cat comes near, such as the SSSCat
- Calming cat pheromone products such as Feliway

Because cats won't normally urinate or defecate where they eat, you can also try feeding your cat on the targeted spot to break the habit. Food dishes can be gradually moved back to their original location after a few weeks, once the association between the target and urination is broken.

You could also try one of the herbal-scented litters that make the litter box more appealing to cats, such as Dr. Elsey's Cat Attract.

If all else fails, it may be necessary to confine the cat to a single room with food and water dishes at one end and the litter box at the other until the bad habit is broken. The cat can gradually be given access to other rooms once he's using his box regularly. Owners should spend plenty of quality time with their cats during this reconditioning period.

References

- Cornell University College of Veterinary Medicine. (2006). "Feline Behavior Problems: House Soiling." Vet.Cornell.edu.
- Cats International. (2007). "The Unabridged Guide to Litterbox Problems." CatsInternational.org.
- Mar Vista Animal Medical Center. (2009). "Feline House Soiling." MarVistaVet.com.Nash, H., DVM, Drs. Foster & Smith. (2010). "Inappropriate Elimination (Urination, Defecation, Spraying) in Cats." PetEducation.com.

Alexandra (Ally) hangs out in her favourite box, Jennifer Copley

Pixel relaxes on my desk, Jennifer Copley

Why do cats scratch furniture and carpets (and how can I stop them from doing this)?

Nimbus uses a scratch post, Jennifer Copley

Contrary to popular belief, cats don't tear up the furniture or carpets to be vindictive or to sharpen their claws. Scratching is actually more akin to grooming than sharpening, as the purpose is often to shed old claw sheaths from the front claws (cats usually chew the sheaths from their back claws).

Cats also have scent glands in their paw pads, so in addition to removing claw sheaths, scratching leaves not only visible marks, but also the feline's personal scent signature to let others know that the item or space is his. Humans can't detect these scent signatures, but another cat can.

Scratching may also act as a stress reliever because it often increases in response to territorial conflicts or other stressors. A cat may vigorously tackle his scratch post or a less appropriate surface when he's frustrated, tense, or anxious.

How to stop cats scratching furniture and carpets

Many cats love nubby upholstery because it mimics the texture of tree bark. Once a cat has claimed a piece of furniture or spot of carpet, it's difficult to change the habit because his personal scent signature will keep luring him back.

Punishment doesn't work with cats – it just increases anxiety, which can lead to more undesirable behaviour. A better strategy is to make the abused surfaces less appealing by covering them with material that cats don't like for a few weeks or so until the habit is broken. Good deterrents include:

- Plastic carpet runner, pointy side up
- Sticky Paws tape
- Sandpaper

Before removing the deterrent, clean the area thoroughly to eradicate any scent traces that will encourage the cat to target the same place again. Using an enzymatic cleaning product such as Nature's Miracle is recommended.

Some people also have luck with herbal deterrents such as Only Natural Pet Herbal Scratch Deterrent or pheromone products such as Feliway. Additional solutions include buying furniture coverings made of thick fabric to protect the targeted item or keeping a blanket over it when not in use.

Provide a good scratch post

Cats need to scratch, so providing at least one scratch post or access to a tree trunk or tree stump is necessary. The post shouldn't be tucked away in some faraway corner of the house, as the cat will be less likely to use it. Placing it near the cat's inappropriate scratching target will ensure that the post gets noticed and may help to redirect the scratching behaviour.

When purchasing or building a scratch post, there are several things to consider. A good scratch post is:

- Sturdy enough that it won't wobble or fall over – if it comes crashing down, the cat may avoid it forever
- Covered with appealing material – sisal twine is usually appreciated, though many cats also like carpet or carpet backing, nubby fabric, burlap, cork, cardboard, or wood
- Tall enough for the cat to stand upright or long enough that he can stretch out horizontally while scratching (ideally at least 3 feet in length or height for an adult cat)

To increase the likelihood that a cat will choose the post over the furniture, purchase or construct a post that has coverings of a similar texture to the cat's favourite piece of furniture or carpeting.

A foster kitten named Hadron uses a scratch post, Jennifer Copley

Make the scratch post appealing

Many cat owners are disappointed when their cats ignore the scratch posts they've purchased or built. To make a scratch post more appealing:

- Place it near the cat's sleep spot.
- Rub a little catnip into it.
- Play with the cat near the post.
- Place the cat's favourite toys on the post.
- Provide treats, praise, and affection when the cat is on or near the post.

Most experts recommend against holding a cat's paws and simulating a scratching motion in the hope of training him to scratch the post. This is ineffective with many cats and may even cause an aversion in some.

References

- Becker, M., DVM, & Willard, J., DVM. (2009). "Why Do Cats Scratch?" CatChannel.com.
- Christensen, W., and the Staff of The Humane Society of the United States. (2002). *The Humane Society of the United States Complete Guide to Cat Care*. New York, NY: St. Martin's Press.
- Estep, D.Q., PhD, & Hetts, S, PhD. (2009). "Why Cats Scratch Things." Animal Behaviour Society, AnimalBehaviour.org.

A cat tree with good scratching surfaces often becomes a prime hangout spot and a hub for feline social interaction, Jennifer Copley

Adding toys to cat trees and scratchposts can make them more appealing, Jennifer Copley

Newly adopted Smokey and Freya learn to use a scratch post, Jennifer Copley

Some cats prefer horizontal scratch surfaces whereas others like a vertical scratcher, Jennifer Copley

Can declawing cats cause behaviour problems?

Most cats will use a cardboard scratcher rather than scratching the furniture if you provide this option, Jennifer Copley

Declawing cats involves not just removing the claws, but also a portion of bone from each front toe, as well as severing the attached tendons and nerves (if this surgery were done on a person, it would involve amputating each finger at the joint closest to the fingernail). A number of studies have found that declawed cats are more likely to develop behaviour problems and be relinquished to shelters as a result.

Declawed cats are more likely to go outside the litter box

According to Dr. Michael Fox, many cats that have been declawed find digging in cat litter too painful and develop a phobia of the litter box as a result. This observation is backed up by the following surveys of cat owners:

- Morgan and Houpt (1989) found that 25% of declawed cats urinated or defecated outside the litter box, compared to 15% of intact cats.
- Yeon et al. (2001) found that 15.4% of cats that had used their litter boxes appropriately before declawing surgery refused to use them after being declawed.

Annie Bruce, author of *Cat Be Good: A Commonsense Approach to Training Your Cat*, has found that of all the calls about declawed cats she has received, "95% ... related to litter box problems, while only 46% of clawed cats had such problems – and most of those were older cats with physical ailments." She also notes that "it's mostly declawed cats that have been prescribed painkillers, anti-depressants, tranquilizers, and steroids."

According to veterinarian Kimberly Harrison, "behavioural problems frequently haunt declawed cats. By far, the commonest thing we see is cats not using the litter box. When cats have stress beyond what they can take, it often shows up as a litter box problem and declawing makes them stress intolerant, in general, for the rest of their lives." Harrison receives up to 12 calls a day regarding litter box problems and has found that 90% of healthy cats that soil around the house have been declawed.

Janet Winikoff, former manager of the Animal Welfare League's adoption program in Alexandria, Virginia, states: "I have seen firsthand the problems associated with declawing. It was not unusual for the shelter to receive surrendered cats that began exhibiting aggressive behaviour and refused to eliminate in the litter box after being declawed. Sadly, these cats were typically considered unadoptable and euthanized."

Other behaviour problems associated with declawing

Deprived of their primary means of defense, some declawed cats become nervous and aggressive. Animal Behaviour Consultant Amy Shojai says that she has advised on many cases in which declawed cats have become biters or developed litter box problems as a result of painful paws. The increased risk for biting is a serious problem because cat bites are more dangerous than cat scratches due to the increased risk of infection.

According to veterinarian Jean Hofve (2001), workers and administrators at various animal shelters have found that declawed cats are more likely to be aggressive. This observation is supported by Yeon et al.'s (2001) study, which found that 17.9% of cats began biting more frequently or harder after they had been declawed.

In addition to the increased risk for litter box problems and aggression, Morgan and Houpt (1989) found that 22% more declawed cats than intact cats were prone to jumping on counters and tables.

Declawed cats are often relinquished to shelters for behaviour problems

Although many veterinarians (who make money from declawing procedures) argue that declawing prevents cats from being surrendered to shelters, the opposite is often true. A study conducted by Patronek et al. (1996) found that of 218 cats that were surrendered to a shelter, 52.4% had been declawed. Given that only about 25% of cats were declawed at the time of the study (this percentage is likely much lower now as the procedure is becoming increasingly unpopular), declawed cats had a surrender rate more than twice as high as that of intact cats.

According to Dr. Fox, "many declawed cats are put up for adoption or are euthanized due to behavioural problems." He says that he has "received a few letters from some cat owners who claim that their cats never developed any problems after being declawed, but ... many more letters to the contrary, so why run the risk?"

Alternatives to declawing cats

Scratching is a natural and necessary behaviour for cats. Alternatives to declawing that enable cats to scratch while saving the furniture include:

- Buying or building a scratch post for the cat
- Trimming the sharp tips of the cat's claws
- Using an emery-board-type scratch post that files down the cat's claws while he scratches
- Using Soft Paws vinyl nail caps
- Using a motion-sensing device that emits a startling burst of air when the cat approaches a forbidden scratching spot
- Spraying a non-toxic pet repellent on the scratch target, such as Grannick's Bitter Apple or Veterinarian's Best Bitter Cherry Spray
- Protecting furniture with covers
- Trying a pheromone spray such as Feliway
- Making the targeted surface unappealing by covering it with Sticky Paws tape, tinfoil, or carpet runner (pointy side up) until the habit is broken

References

- Bruce, A., & Dodman, N.H. (n.d.). "FAQs About Litter Box Problems and Declawing." GoodCatsWearBlack.com.
- Fox, M.W. (n.d.). "Say No! To Declawing Cats." TwoBitDog.com/DrFox/.
- Hofve, J. (2001). "FAQs on Declawing and Feline Scratching Behavior." PawProject.com.
- Landsberg, G.M. (1991). "Cat Owners' Attitudes Toward Declawing. *Anthrozoos, 4*: 192-197.
- Morgan M., & Houpt, K.A. (1989). "Feline Behavior Problems: The Influence of Declawing. *Anthrozoos, 3*: 50-53.
- Patronek, G.J., et al. (1996). "Risk Factors for Relinquishment of Cats to an Animal Shelter." *Journal of the American Veterinary Medical Association, 209*: 582-588.
- Perry, T. (1988). "Declawing: Behavior Modification or Destructive Surgery?" *Animal Issues, 29*(4).
- Yeon, S.C., et al. (2001). "Attitudes of Owners Regarding Tendonectomy and Onychectomy in Cats." *Journal of the American Veterinary Medical Association, 218*: 43-47.

Chapter 10: Cats and Kittens

Resident cats Sage and Smokey care for a young orphaned foster kitten, Jennifer Copley

Will tom cats kill kittens?

The reason why I can't get any work done: Smokey hangs out with 5 foster kittens on and around my mouse pad, Jennifer Copley

Many people mistakenly believe that tom cats will always kill kittens, if given the chance, to secure more mating opportunities. However, tom cats are more likely to ignore their own kittens or even take on a paternal role than to murder their offspring, and they often ignore kittens sired by other toms rather than killing them as well.

Some tom cats will actually protect and nurture their kittens if they have access, though they may not get the opportunity because females often drive males away from the nesting area once the kittens are born.

Neutered males are far less likely to show aggression toward kittens, regardless of whether they are related to them. Our resident adult males take on a nurturing role with our foster kittens.

A litter of kittens can have more than one father

The ability to produce a litter of kittens fathered by more than one tom cat is called superfecundation. A female cat in heat attracts many different males. If she has a particular preference, she will only mate with one tom, waiting for him to recover after prior matings rather than seeking the attentions of other males while he's incapacitated. But many female cats will accommodate a broader circle of admirers, so their ova may be fertilized by the sperm of various males, producing a litter of kittens that look very different from one another.

Superfecundation is particularly likely to occur in urban and suburban areas where cats have higher population densities, which increases the number of male respondents to the call of a female cat in heat.

In addition to the potential for superfecundation, some female cats will actually go into heat and be impregnated while already pregnant, a phenomenon known as superfetation. In this case, a mother cat may simultaneously carry two litters at different stages of development. The less developed litter may be born prematurely along with the more advanced litter, which usually results in death for the premature kittens, but if they're lucky, they manage to hang on for the full term and are born 2-6 weeks later. This places a significant burden on the nursing mother because she suddenly has a lot of kittens to cope with all at once, though many cats deal effectively with these large, staggered litters.

Because of superfecundation and superfetation, several tom cats may be fathers to a single litter.

Sage hugs a foster kitten, Jennifer Copley

Male cats in feral colonies have been observed bringing food to mothers and kittens and defending them against people and other animals. Some males even take over mothering duties if their kittens are orphaned or the mother is incompetent.

A pair of very-different-looking kittens from the same litter, Jennifer Copley

It's very uncommon for a male to kill his own kittens. The small size, erratic movements, and high-pitched voices of kittens occasionally cause an adult male or a female that has never had kittens to mistake a kitten for prey, but this is very rare.

Tom cat responses to kittens fathered by other males vary from one cat to the next. In some cases, toms will kill another male's kittens as a lion would kill cubs to bring a female into heat sooner, particularly if there are other males in the area and competition is intense. However, they're more likely to tolerate or ignore kittens sired by other toms, though adult feral males may drive juveniles away from the group when they reach sexual maturity.

Because of the risk posed by strange males, feline fathers may run them off or groups of females will work together to defend against them.

Sage washes Fluffasaurus Rex, Jennifer Copley

Smokey hugs an orphaned foster kitten named Leo, Jennifer Copley

Sage hangs out with an unrelated foster kitten that looks a lot like him, Jennifer Copley

Sage and Smokey with a foster kitten on my desk, Jennifer Copley

Sage with Princess Fluffington, Jennifer Copley

Smokey with another foster kitten, Jennifer Copley

References

- Hartwell, Sarah. (1996). "Cats That Kill Kittens." MessyBeast.com.
- Morris, Desmond. (1987). *Catlore*. London, UK: Jonathan Cape Ltd.

Will handling newborn kittens make their mother reject them?

A newborn kitten, Mrmiscellaneous, Wikimedia Commons, Public Domain

Contrary to popular belief, touching newborn kittens is unlikely to cause their mother to reject them, and handling kittens regularly from week 2 onward will make them friendlier and less fearful as adults, provided the handling is gentle. General handling guidelines are as follows:

- Always wash hands thoroughly with soap and water before touching kittens to avoid introducing germs (their immature immune systems can't handle bad microbes).
- Begin handling and stroking kittens regularly (but for just a couple of minutes at a time) during the second week after birth.
- Gradually increase handling times as kittens grow older.
- Hold kittens close to the nest, within view of their mother.
- Supervise older children's interactions with kittens and don't allow very young children to handle them.
- Don't attempt to handle kittens if the mother doesn't appear calm and relaxed.
- If the mother shows signs of agitation when a kitten is removed, return the kitten immediately.

Reference: ASPCA Virtual Pet Behaviorist. (2009). "Socializing Your Kitten." ASPCABehavior.org.

Why do mother cats move kittens?

A nursing mother cat in Greece, Charles Nadeau, Flickr, Creative Commons 2.0

Feral cats often move their kittens if they feel that the nesting site has become unsafe for some reason, and domestic cats have the same urge to hide their offspring from predators and to avoid staying too long in one place where their kittens might be noticed.

Causes of kitten moving

A mother cat is most likely to move her kittens during the first few weeks after they are born. Kitten moving indicates that the mother is nervous, either because she's inexperienced, she feels that the nest site is unsafe, or both. Things that may trigger the urge to move include lack of privacy, noise, or bright lights.

While some cats are fine with attention and handling of their kittens shortly after birth, a nervous mother, particularly if it's her first litter, may find this stressful. For the first few days after the birth, keep interaction to a minimum, just checking to make sure that mom and kittens are healthy and that mom cat's food dishes are full and her litter box is clean. If the mother appears nervous or agitated with people around or has already moved her kittens once, extend the minimal-contact time to the first couple of weeks.

How to reduce the likelihood of kitten moving

During their first weeks of life, kittens can't regulate their body temperature, so they depend on their mother for warmth. If a mother cat moves her kittens frequently, there is a risk that they may become chilled.

To reduce the likelihood of frequent kitten moving, provide a dry, clean, cozy nesting box in a quiet, low-traffic corner of the home free from bright lights and draughts. A suitable box can be purchased or made from cardboard, wood, or a plastic storage container. The box should be around 1.5-2 feet square (depending on the size of the mother cat), with a door on one side and a removable lid. Artificial fleece blankets or tight-weave towels make good bedding (avoid terry cloth, which can snag kittens' claws).

Pay attention to the mother's body language and behaviour when handling kittens. Within 1 or 2 weeks after birth, most mothers will allow handling if the kittens are held briefly and kept in the mother's sight at all times (calmer mothers will be comfortable with trusted people handling their kittens even earlier). Handling kittens from week 2 onward is recommended if the mother will allow it because this helps socialize the kittens to humans. However, if the mother seems agitated when a kitten is held or touched, it should be returned to the nest immediately.

Children shouldn't visit or handle kittens unless they are able to remain quiet and calm and hold the kittens gently.

If the mother moves her kittens, leave them in the new place she has chosen if possible (unless the new nest presents a safety hazard). Turn on the heat in the new room to prevent the kittens from becoming chilled, avoid using bright lights near the new nesting site, and leave the mother and her kittens alone until she has settled down – interaction right after a move may provoke another move.

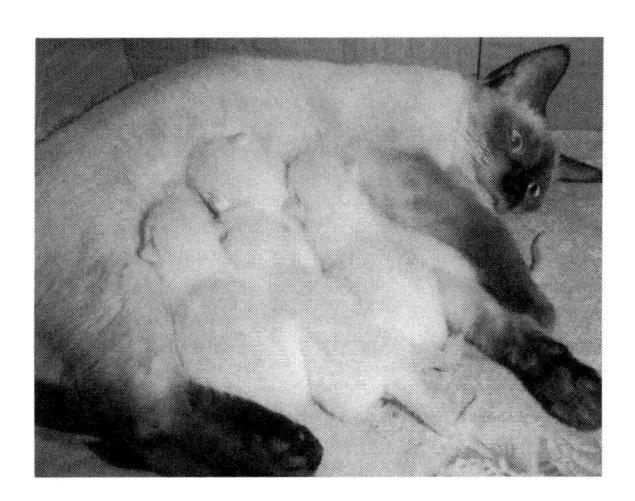

A Siamese cat with kittens, Black Zero, Flickr, Creative Commons 2.0

References

- East Bay SPCA. (2009). "Stray Cats and Kittens." EastBaySPCA.org.
- Eldredge, D.M., DVM; Carlson, D.G., DVM; Carlson, L.D., DVM; & Giffin, J.M., MD. (2008). *Cat Owner's Home Veterinary Handbook, Third Edition*. Wiley Publishing, Inc.
- Merck & Co., Inc., Eds. Kahn, C.M., BA, MA, & Line, S., DVM, PhD, Dipl. ACVB. (2007). *The Merck/Merial Manual for Pet Health, Home Edition*.
- Rice, D., DVM. (1997). *The Complete Book of Cat Breeding*. Hauppage, NY: Barron's Educational Series.
- Schelling, C., Dr. (2010). "Veterinary Topics: Feline Reproduction: Kittens Birth to Weaning." CatHealth.com.

At what age can cats start having kittens?

A mother cat with kittens, Freestocks.org, Flickr, Public Domain

Although their bodies continue to mature throughout the first year of life, some cats of both genders can begin breeding as early as 4 or 5 months of age. However, the majority of female cats experience their first heat at around 6 months of age, though anywhere from 5-12 months is normal for most breeds, while many male cats can sire a litter by 5 months of age.

Chapter 11: Cats and Dogs

A dog waits patiently for his owner, Jennifer Copley

Can cats and dogs be friends?

Cat and dog, Petteri Sulonen, Flickr, Creative Commons 2.0

Many people want to have more than one pet, but they are concerned about potential conflicts, particularly between cats and dogs. However, the findings of a study conducted by Professor Joseph Terkel and graduate student Neta-li Feuerstein of Tel Aviv University indicate that cats and dogs can get along well, provided certain conditions are met.

Conflicts between cats and dogs often result from crossed signals. For example, a dog wags her tail when happy, whereas a cat with a swishing tail is angry. A dog may perceive the moving tail as a friendly, welcoming signal, but the cat has actually been warning the dog off and feels threatened by the dog's continued advance, so he lashes out.

Despite these differences in body language, Terkel and Feuerstein found that in nearly two-thirds of multi-pet households that included both cats and dogs, the pets were good friends. In many cases they had even learned to read one another's signals, thereby overcoming their cultural differences. In other words, dogs had learned to speak "cat" and vice-versa. The researchers also found that cats and dogs in harmonious households often snuggled together while sleeping.

Cats and dogs were good friends in 65% of households included in the research, and in another 25% of multi-pet households, they had established a peaceable indifference to one another. They were hostile and aggressive toward each another in just 10% of multi-pet homes.

How to increase the likelihood that cats and dogs will become friends

The Terkel and Feuerstein research findings indicate that cats and dogs are most likely to become friends when the following conditions are met:

- The cat is adopted first.
- The cat is under 6 months old when she meets the dog.
- The dog is adopted at less than a year old.

However, there have been plenty of positive cat-dog relationships established even when these conditions were not met. To increase the likelihood that pets will become friends, it's important to handle the introductions properly, particularly if both pets are adults.

Adopters can maximize the likelihood of a successful integration by choosing a shelter dog that has prior experience with cats, or a shelter cat that has lived with dogs in the past.

Reference: ScienceDaily.com. (9 September 2008). "Dogs and cats can live in perfect harmony in the home, if introduced the right way" (summary of the Terkel and Feuerstein study). ScienceDaily.com.

How should I introduce a new dog to my cat?

A dog in the snow, Jennifer Copley

The key to a smooth introduction is to ensure that the cat doesn't feel threatened. Dogs are natural predators of cats, so unless they've had prior positive experiences with dogs, all but the most laid back cats will feel threatened by the introduction of a new dog. The way in which the two pets are introduced can have a significant effect on their future interactions, so it's important to do the right things when you first put the two animals together.

Choosing a dog

There is a risk that a new dog will attack the cat. Dogs that have lived with cats previously usually get along well with them, but a dog with no prior cat experience may behave unpredictably. In the case of a puppy under 3 months old, the risk is relatively low, but with a bigger dog, you'll need to ensure the cat's safety.

If you're adopting a dog from an animal shelter, you can request that the staff check the dog's behaviour around cats before you make your final decision. If adopting the dog from another owner, ask the owner about any prior interactions the dog has had with cats. Ideally, the prospective adoptee has lived with cats before, has a gentle nature, or is very young. A dog that has been raised with cats is unlikely to attack them.

If possible, start with a trial adoption to make sure the dog is not inclined to be violent toward your cat before making a final decision.

Introducing a new dog to your cat

Keep the two animals separate until they are used to one another. Use a baby gate or some other type of barrier to confine the dog to one area of the house or apartment – a room or two. This will enable the cat to take the initiative in approaching the dog, which is important, as the cat is the one that will feel threatened.

Once the cat comfortably approaches the dog, the gate or barrier can be removed, but the first interactions should be supervised. Monitor their behaviour together during the initial meetings. Don't let the dog bark, chase, or lunge at the cat, as this could destroy the potential for a good relationship. Use a short leash if the dog is excitable and watch the situation closely. Attacks can happen swiftly, and because she is much smaller, the cat can be seriously hurt during a brief scuffle.

The cat will usually only attack if the dog corners her, so preventing the dog from cornering the cat will reduce the likelihood of the dog getting scratched. In a worst-case scenario, the cat may scratch the dog's eyes, but corneal lacerations, when treated by a veterinarian, usually heal without any permanent effects.

When stopping the dog from chasing or barking, use commands or restrain him gently; don't punish the dog because this can create a negative association. (the cat shouldn't be punished for growling, hissing, or swiping at the dog for the same reason). Reward both pets with treats and praise for interacting positively or even just being in the same room without behaving badly toward one another.

Don't leave the dog and the cat alone together until you're sure they're completely comfortable with one another. Dogs and cats can become the best of friends as long as the introductions are handled carefully.

Introducing a new cat to your dog

If you have a resident dog and the cat is the newcomer, all the same strategies should be used. The main difference is that the resident dog has established his territory and may guard food and other things within this territory, which could present a risk to the cat. In this case, the dog should be retrained, if possible, to share his space. If this doesn't work, the animals may need to be permanently kept apart using a gate or other barrier. However, most cats and dogs can learn to peacefully share a territory.

References

- Ohio State University College of Veterinary Medicine: "Introducing New Pets." IndoorPet.OSU.edu.
- Feinman, J., VMD, CVH. "Introducing New Pets to Resident Pets." HomeVet.com.

Which cat breeds get along best with dogs?

Maine Coon, Heikki Siltala, Catza.net, Creative Commons 3.0

Birman, Heikki Siltala, Catza.net, Creative Commons 3.0

Animal Planet has rated cat breeds based on how well they tend to get along with other pets. Of course, there will always be exceptions because not every cat of a given breed will have all the characteristics of that breed, and individual cats may have had positive or negative experiences with dogs.

The highest compatibility ratings went to the Manx and its long-haired counterpart, the Cymric, which received scores of 9 out of 10 for their ability to integrate within multi-pet households. Manx and Cymric cats are tailless or have very short, stubby tails. Many cats of these breeds are described as doglike due to their willingness to play fetch and travel in vehicles. These cats tend to be relatively adaptable in general and less traumatized by change than cats of most other breeds.

The following cat breeds received a relatively high score of 8 out of 10 for their ability to get along with other pets:

- American Curl
- American Shorthair
- Birman
- Exotic Shorthair
- Himalayan
- Maine Coon
- Ocicat

- Persian
- Ragdoll
- Siberian
- Sphynx

This is quite a varied group, ranging from the ultra-intelligent Sphynx to the laid-back Persian to the hardy American Shorthair. What they have in common is that they all tend to be relatively easy going and tolerant.

Cat breeds that may have difficulty getting along with other pets

Animal Planet gave the following cat breeds ratings of just 5 out of 10 for their ability to live happily with other pets:

- Abyssinian
- Balinese
- Burmese
- Colourpoint Shorthair
- Devon Rex
- Egyptian Mau
- Javanese
- Korat
- Oriental
- Russian Blue
- Siamese
- Singapura
- Somali

Many of these breeds are derived from the Siamese, a highly intelligent but sensitive breed. Others, like the Korat and the Russian Blue, tend to be timid and prone to startling, so they may have difficulty with rambunctious dogs.

The Cornish Rex, a curly-coated breed, received a score of just 4 out of 10, and the Bengal, a wild-cat hybrid, came in at the bottom with a rating of 3 out of 10. Although these breeds may have difficulty adapting to multi-pet households as adults, if they are introduced as kittens (ideally at around 12-16 weeks of age), they have a much higher likelihood of integrating well.

Some cat fanciers disagree with Animal Planet ratings. In particular, many fans of the Devon and Cornish Rex say these are dog-friendly breeds, as long as the dogs they live with are cat-friendly.

Reference: Animal Planet. (2010). "Cat Breed Selector." Animal.Discovery.com.

Which dog breeds get along best with cats?

Golden Retriever, Jennifer Copley

Most dogs are good with cats if they have lived with them from an early age, but some dog breeds tend to be particularly cat-friendly. Animal Planet's top-rated dog breeds for cat-friendliness include:

- American Cocker Spaniel
- Beagle
- Bloodhound
- Chinese Crested Dog
- English Cocker Spaniel
- English Springer Spaniel

- Field Spaniel
- Golden Retriever
- Labrador Retriever
- Newfoundland
- Nova Scotia Duck Tolling Retriever
- Old English Sheepdog
- Samoyed

Spaniels, Retrievers, Beagles, and other gentle breeds tend to be particularly good with cats, though there are exceptions to this rule.

Dog breeds that are bad with cats

PetPlace's Irreverent Vet asserts that certain dog breeds such as Greyhounds, Pit Bulls, and Parson Russell Terriers are more likely to be bad with cats. This doesn't mean that all dogs of these breeds are hostile toward cats, but there is a higher likelihood of conflicts.

Greyhounds

Racing greyhounds have been trained to chase and may have trouble overcoming this conditioning, but according to Greyhound expert Debbie Buxcey, with proper "detraining," 90% of greyhounds can be taught to accept resident cats as members of their packs, though they will probably still chase unknown cats if they have the opportunity.

Pit Bulls

The Irreverent Vet has seen more cats injured and killed by Pit Bulls than by dogs of any other breed. However, it's usually bad owners rather than bad natures that cause Pit Bulls to turn mean.

According to Karen Delise, Director of Research for the National Canine Research Council, Pit Bulls have been a favourite of criminals who raise dogs for fighting and other aggressive purposes, and these dogs usually suffer severe abuse and neglect. In addition, media hype has demonized the breed. However, there are many responsible Pit Bull owners who socialize their dogs properly, treat them well, and don't let them escape and roam. There are also plenty of photos available online showing Pit Bulls snuggling with cats, so these dogs have the potential to be cat-friendly.

A friendly Pit Bull, Jennifer Copley

Pit Bulls that are well-socialized and cared for tend to be trustworthy and good-natured, and although Pit Bulls that have been poorly socialized, abused, or neglected may be particularly dangerous, the same could be said of many other dog breeds.

Pit Bull Rescue Central offers advice on how to integrate Pit Bulls within cat-owning households, noting that although some Pit Bulls have too strong a prey drive to live with cats, most will be cat-friendly if they are well trained and introduced in a positive way. If adopting an adult Pit Bull, the organization recommends asking whether the dog has been tested with cats prior to bringing him home.

Parson Russell Terriers/Jack Russell Terriers

The Irreverent Vet notes that a number of cats have been killed or injured by Parson Russell Terriers, and Terriers in general are over-represented among Animal Planet's lowest-ranked dogs for cat-friendliness. Terriers were originally bred to hunt, so many are inclined to chase cats, but some Terriers can learn to control themselves, particularly with positive early socialization.

Other dog breeds that may not get along with cats

The following dog breeds received Animal Planet ratings of just 1 or 2 out of 5 for cat-friendliness:

- Airedale Terrier
- Alaska Malamute
- American Staffordshire Terrier
- Australian Cattledog
- Basenji
- Beauceron
- Bedlington Terrier
- Border Collie
- Cairn Terrier
- German Pinscher
- Irish Terrier
- Kerry Blue Terrier
- Lakeland Terrier
- Manchester Terrier
- Miniature Pinscher
- Neapolitan Mastiff
- Norwegian Elkhound
- Parson Russell Terrier
- Pharoah Hound
- Plott
- Redbone Coonhound
- Rhodesian Ridgeback
- Rottweiler
- Shiba Inu
- Skye Terrier
- Smooth Fox Terrier
- Weimaraner
- Welsh Terrier
- Wire Fox Terrier
- Yorkshire Terrier

In some cases, conflicts with these breeds are usually benign. For example, Border Collies have a tendency to herd cats and other pets, and although they are unlikely to hurt them, cats may find the constant chasing traumatic.

With other breeds, the risk may be relatively high. According to the Weimaraner Club of Kansas City, a significant percentage of Weimaraners will kill cats if given the opportunity.

However, even the least cat-friendly dog breeds can become best friends with cats if they are raised with them. Also, there are individuals within each breed that behave differently from the breed standard.

References

- Animal Planet. (2011). "Dog Breed Selector." Animal.Discovery.com.
- Buxcey, D. (2008). "Detraining Greyhounds to Live with Cats." Greyhounds4u.co.uk.
- Delise, K. (2007). *The Pit Bull Placebo: The Media, Myths and Politics of Canine Aggression*. NationalCanineResearchCouncil.com.
- Devine, M, & Earle-Bridges, M. (2007). *Border Collies: A Complete Pet Owner's Manual*. Hauppage, NY: Barron's Educational Series, Inc.
- Irreverent Vet. (2010). "The Irreverent Vet Speaks out on Dog Breeds That Are Bad with Cats." PetPlace.com.
- Pit Bull Rescue Central. (2010). "Cat/Dog Households." PBRC.net.
- Weimaraner Club of Greater Kansas City. (2009). "FAQ About Weimaraners." WCGKC.org.

Bernese Mountain Dog (not included in the Animal Planet rankings, but these dogs tend to be calm and laid back, and many people say they get along well with cats, though socialization will play a role), Jennifer Copley

How can I stop my cat from attacking my dog?

A cat attacking a dog, Bruno Caimi, Flickr, Creative Commons 2.0

A cat is more likely to bluff by growling, hissing, and puffing up than to launch a full-scale attack against a dog, but there are situations in which a cat will be actively aggressive.

The most common cause of cat attacks on dogs is defensive aggression – a fearful cat may launch a pre-emptive strike. Another cause is territorial aggression. If the dog invades the cat's space or begins making use of the cat's resources (beds, food dishes, etc.), the cat may feel a need to defend his territory.

In some cases, a cat will attack because a dog behaves like prey, acting fearful and running away. Other times the cat is just playing; a wiggling dog tail looks like a cat toy, and the cat pounces, after which the play may get out of hand.

Preventing cat-to-dog aggression

You can reduce the risk of feline aggression by:

- Spaying or neutering your pets
- Using relaxing pet pheromones such as Feliway for cats
- Preventing the dog from getting into the cat's food or litter box to reduce territorial defensiveness
- Putting a bell on the cat to give the dog a warning so he can avoid confrontation
- Giving the cat a place to escape (a tall cat tree or cat tunnel) to reduce the likelihood of aggression due to a panicked fight-or-flight response
- Rewarding the cat with treats, affection, and praise when he behaves calmly in the presence of the dog
- Providing each animal with his own toys, food bowls, and bed
- Using tall baby gates, pet gates, or other barriers to create permanent safe spaces for the dog in extreme cases of feline aggression

If the aggression is just playfulness getting out of hand rather than territoriality or fearful defensiveness, attaching a leash to the dog's collar can be beneficial. The dog will drag the leash around, and the cat will be more inclined to attack the moving leash than the dog.

Feline predatory aggression toward dogs

Cats don't usually show predatory aggression toward large dogs, but they may view very small dogs or puppies as prey. However, this is uncommon, and when it occurs, the risk diminishes over time as the cat matures and the dog grows larger.

If your cat is behaving predatorially, the puppy or small dog should be protected by separating your pets with tall baby gates, keeping them in different rooms with a door shut between them, or putting the dog inside an upended baby playpen when you can't directly supervise their interactions.

Misdirected cat-to-dog aggression

A cat will occasionally begin to victimize a dog due to misdirected aggression. The cat, frustrated because he's seen an animal outside a window that he can't get to, attacks the dog. If the dog behaves like a victim by running away, the cat may continue to treat him as a scapegoat.

If misdirected aggression is the cause of bullying behaviour, you may have to block access to the window or windows or use a product such as Sticky Paws tape on the windowsills to keep the cat from sitting there.

If your pets have developed a victim-aggressor association, they may have to be separated for days (or even weeks) until the association is broken. This can be done using tall baby gates or some other barrier to separate two areas of the house.

How to break up a fight between an aggressive cat and a small dog

A big dog that is being harassed by a cat can usually take care of himself, but a small dog is more likely to be injured or traumatized. If a fight breaks out, the following strategies can be used to break it up:

- Make a loud noise – drop a heavy book or bang two objects together.
- Spray the combatants with water or toss water over them.
- Protect your hand with an oven mitt and place a barrier between them (this could be anything from a cookie sheet to a large book or a pillow).
- Throw a thick blanket over the combatants so that you're less likely to be clawed or bitten when you break up the fight.
- Wrap the aggressor in a blanket or thick towel and bundle him out of the room. Keep him in another room until he has calmed down.

When breaking up cat-and-dog fights, there are two important things to remember. First, yelling isn't recommended, as this tends to increase aggression rather than diminishing it. Second, cats don't respond well to punishment. In fact, punishment is likely to increase aggression in cats, as it makes them fearful and defensive. Rewarding the cat for good behaviour is far more effective than punishing bad behaviour.

Once the fight is over, ignore the cat (or both animals if the fault was mutual rather than one-sided) for at least half an hour. This signals displeasure and doesn't reward the bad behaviour with extra attention.

Reference: Shojai, A.D. (2005). PETiQuette: *Solving Behavior Problems in Your Multi-Pet Household*. New York, NY: M. Evans and Company, Inc.

How can I stop my dog from attacking my cat?

Cat and dog, Katlene Niven, Flickr, Creative Commons 2.0

Dogs usually attack cats due to either predatory instinct or status-related issues. A dog that was not socialized with cats as a puppy may view them as prey, particularly if a timid cat runs and this motion triggers the dog's chase reflex.

A dog may also feel that he has lost status either when a new cat is brought home, or a resident cat comes home after a visit to the vet. Also, when a dominant pet becomes ill or dies, other household pets may scramble to fill the status void, triggering fights.

Dogs are more inclined to abuse shy, timid cats. Bullying behaviours can range from posturing to full chase and attack.

Preventing dog-to-cat aggression

Strategies for reducing the risk of dog-to-cat aggression include:

- Neutering or spaying the dog to decrease aggressiveness
- Saying "no" in a calm, firm voice whenever the dog is eyeing the cat as though he plans to attack
- Keeping pets in separate rooms or areas of the house blocked off with tall baby gates when you can't directly supervise them
- Muzzling the dog in the presence of the cat until you're sure that he can control himself
- Providing the cat with a tall cat tree or other place of refuge
- Using a pheromone product such as D.A.P. (Dog Appeasing Pheromone) to make the dog calmer
- Giving each animal his own food and water bowls and toys to reduce territorial aggression
- Placing the cat's food bowls in an area where he can escape easily if ambushed
- Taking the dog to obedience training

Countering predatory aggression in dogs

Some dogs have great difficulty giving up the immediate gratification of the chase even for treats or praise. In such cases, a more comprehensive counter-conditioning strategy must be used to reduce the dog's predatory urges.

Supervise encounters between the dog and the cat and keep the dog on a leash to stop him from running at the cat. Reward the leashed dog with treats or praise whenever he's in the same room as the cat. Do this regularly for 1-2 weeks and then occasionally thereafter to maintain the positive association.

Keep the animals separated using baby gates or closed doors when you aren't around to supervise, and keep the dog leashed in the presence of the cat until you're sure that he can control himself. Eventually, the dog will react to the cat's presence by looking at you in the hope of praise or a treat rather than chasing the cat.

How to break up a fight between a dog and a cat

Ideally, fights should be prevented altogether, but if a fight does break out, it needs to be stopped as soon as possible because the cat could be severely injured, and the dog may sustain scratches to his eyes or worse injuries if he is small.

When intervening in a fight, keep yourself as safe as possible. Low-risk strategies for breaking up fights between a cat and a large dog include:

- Pulling on the dog's leash if that's available
- Grabbing the dog's back legs and pulling him backwards wheelbarrow style (be sure to keep moving backwards until he's calmed down)
- Using something long with a soft end to separate the combatants, such as a broom
- Throwing water over the dog
- Making a loud noise (i.e., banging two pots together)

If the dog is small, you can just throw a blanket over the combatants or wrap the dog in a blanket or thick towel and carry him out of the room.

Pulling the dog away by his collar is not recommended, as he may whip around and bite you in the heat of the moment. Yelling is also a bad idea, as human shouts may increase aggression rather than decreasing it.

After the fight, ignore the aggressor (or both pets if they have been equally culpable) for at least half an hour. This signals displeasure and ensures that you don't inadvertently reward the bad behaviour with extra attention.

Reference: Shojai, A.D. (2005). *PETiQuette: Solving Behavior Problems in Your Multi-Pet Household*. New York, NY: M. Evans and Company, Inc.

Chapter 12: Miscellaneous Cat Quirks

A curious cat on a fence, Jennifer Copley

Why do cats sometimes appear to be grimacing with their mouths open?

Smokey, Jennifer Copley

Many animals (including horses, buffalo, llamas, and tigers) have a sensory organ called the Jacobson organ (or vomeronasal organ) that enables them to gather more information about scents through the roofs of their mouths. A cat using this organ will open his mouth and make an odd face, as though he is sneering, grimacing, or frozen with his mouth slightly open as he draws air into the organ to check it. Many people mistakenly assume that the cat is disgusted when he does this, because he may wrinkle up his nose in a way that a human would if encountering an unpleasant smell. This "grimace" is known as the Flehmen response.

The Jacobson organ, which is connected to areas of the brain associated with sexual, social, and feeding behaviours, is most often used by male cats to determine the sexual status of local females – in other words, to discover whether they are fertile and ovulating by the scent of their urine. However, both female and male cats display the Flehmen response when encountering a variety of scents.

It has been speculated that in addition to determining whether females are in heat, cats may be able to gather information about the physiological states of many different of animals using the Flehmen response, which can assist with predatory activities. Also, because cats may engage in the Flehmen response when encountering interesting plant scents such as catnip, this extra sense organ may have broader applications, but more research is required to identify all its uses.

References

- Tabor, R. (2005). *100 Ways to Understand Your Cat*. Cincinnati, OH: David & Charles.
- Case, L.P. (2003). *The Cat: Its Behaviour, Nutrition, and Health*. Ames, Iowa: Iowa State Press.

Why do cats make sudden mad dashes around the house?

A foster kitten about to dash, Jennifer Copley

A cat that appears perfectly calm will suddenly go on a tear, running around the house as though being chased by a predator or chasing prey. Those who have never seen this behaviour may worry that the cat is hallucinating or suffering a fit, but this activity usually indicates boredom rather than illness.

Cypress in a contemplative mood, Jennifer Copley

Housebound cats, while far safer than their outdoor counterparts, are more likely to dash because they lack opportunities to hunt. The dash may occur out of the blue (chasing "ghost prey") or be an overreaction to mild stimuli, such as a movement or sound.

Some bored cats will even launch a mock attack on a human companion or another pet, or generally make nuisances of themselves to provoke irritation so they can overreact and run away as though being chased by an angry adversary.

To keep indoor cats from becoming frustrated and hyperactive or listless:

- Buy or make cat toys and play with your cat more often.
- Purchase or build a cat enclosure or fence so your cat can safely spend time outside.
- Leash train your cat and take her for walks outdoors.
- Purchase or build a cat tree to provide more indoor recreation opportunities.

Reference: Morris, D. (1987). *Catlore*. London, UK: Jonathan Cape Ltd.

Why do cats knead or paddle with their paws?

Many cats make kneading motions (also referred to as paddling) with their paws, especially when they're sitting on people's laps. This involves pressing one paw down and then the other in an alternating motion, spreading the toes with each push. Some people jokingly refer to this activity as "making bread" because it resembles kneading a batch of dough.

Kittens knead when nursing to stimulate milk flow. Because people are much larger and they provide food and care for their cats, domestic cats are like permanent kittens with humans as their surrogate parents. When cats snuggle up with a warm person they love, they can relive the contentment of being a kitten by kneading, often purring at the same time.

Wild cats also use a kneading motion when softening material to make a nest, and some cats will knead soft fabrics in anticipation of lying down to sleep. Kneading or paddling is perfectly natural (not a sign of anxiety or other psychological problems).

Some people dislike kneading if cats don't keep their claws fully sheathed. Trimming the sharp tips of their claws can prevent accidental scratches.

Reference: Tabor, R. (2005). *100 Ways to Understand Your Cat*. Cincinnati, OH: David & Charles.

Sleepy kitten fight between Nimbus and Rambler, Jennifer Copley

Why does a tom cat bite a female's neck while mating?

Mating cats, Muppaphone, Flickr, Creative Commons 2.0

Many people find this behaviour (along with the shrieks of female cats) alarming because it gives the impression of a forced encounter, but neck biting is actually a defensive action on the male's part. Although females choose their mates and mating is voluntary, the male needs to protect himself in case she decides to attack him for some reason while he's in a vulnerable position. Kittens have an instinct to stay still when held by the scruff of the neck, and adult cats maintain this instinct to some degree, so holding the scruff of the neck reduces the likelihood of attack.

It was once believed that a female cat shrieks after mating because the spines on a male cat's penis (which induce ovulation in female cats) cause pain during withdrawal, but experts now think that the shriek is a warning gesture. The female, in a vulnerable position because the male has his teeth clamped on the back of her neck, lets him know that he'd better not take advantage by doing anything aggressive. Given that mating cats often don't know one another beforehand, taking a few precautions is sensible in case they've chosen an unusually volatile partner.

References

- Morris, D. (1986). *Catwatching*. Three Rivers Press: Random House.
- Seidensticker, J., & Lumpkin, S. (2006). *Cats: Smithsonian Q&A: The Ultimate Question and Answer Book*. Washington, DC: Smithsonian Books.

Why do some cats play with water?

Freya at 12 weeks of age, Jennifer Copley

Many cats (particularly wild-cat hybrids such as the Bengal) play with standing water in bowls, toilets, and bathtubs, or water running from faucets. This water play probably arises from an instinct for self-preservation.

When a cat dips her paw in her drinking water or splashes around in it, she may be testing for hidden dangers. Is the water too hot? Is there something scary in it? Although cats have very good distance vision, at close range their eyesight isn't as strong, so they tend to rely on their sensitive noses and paw pads to answer questions about their immediate environments.

Many cats prefer to drink from (and play with) water running from faucets or fountain-type water bowls just as wild animals prefer to drink from streams rather than ponds. Cats are probably attracted to running water because it tends to harbour fewer contaminants than standing water.

Cats may also play with water for the enjoyment of seeing the ripples form and spread, and in some cases the attraction goes beyond simply dipping a paw or splashing around a little.

There are cat breeds that are naturally drawn to water, such as the Turkish Van (known as the swimming cat). Many Turkish Vans will actually dive into pools or lakes or join their owners in the shower.

How to stop cats playing with water

Water play can be exasperating because owners have to clean up the resulting mess. To reduce or eliminate water mess, you can cut a hole in a large clean plastic milk container, a couple of inches above the bottom, and provide water in the container (the hole should be large enough to accommodate the cat's whiskers). Although many cats don't mind drinking from a plastic jug, some dislike the taste of water that has been in contact with plastic, so not all cats will take to this.

You can also put your cat's water dish on a large plastic tray with sides a few inches high to contain the mess.

If a cat has suddenly begun spilling her water after a traumatic event such as the introduction of a new pet or moving house, the behaviour may be a stress reliever or a request for attention and reassurance.

Providing extra attention and playtime can be beneficial in such cases.

References

- Heinzen, D., TNT Purrfect Persians. (2007). "Water Bottle Tips." Chocolate Cat Fanciers, ChocolateCats.com.
- Moore, A. (2007). *The Cat Behavior Answer Book*. North Adams, MA: Storey Publishing.
- Shojai, A. (n.d.). "Ask Amy: Cat Play in Water." About.com.

Why do cats chew on their claws?

Leo, Jennifer Copley

Nail biting in cats is usually nothing to worry about. Cats do this to remove old claw sheaths, particularly on their back feet (it's easier for them to shed claw sheaths on their front feet by scratching rough surfaces such as tree bark or scratch posts). Like other aspects of grooming, claw chewing can become excessive, indicating an anxiety problem, but in most cases the behaviour is completely harmless.

Why do cats gravitate to people who fear or dislike them?

Some people assume that cats enjoy tormenting those who don't like them because they always seem to approach the one cat hater in the room, but this mistaken belief arises from a misunderstanding of feline communication. People who like cats tend to stare at them, but cats perceive a direct stare as a challenge, particularly from people they don't know well. Cats often make a beeline for the one person in the room who isn't staring at them, which is often the person who fears or dislikes cats.

Reference: Schneck, M., & Caravan, J. (1990). *Cat Facts*. New York, NY: Barnes & Noble Inc.

Curious Nimbus, Jennifer Copley

A Picatso portrait, Jennifer Copley

Why do cats purr?

Nimbus and Rambler sleeping on my lap, Jennifer Copley

Purring would not have evolved unless it provided a survival advantage. Most people assume that cats purr only to express contentment, but this doesn't explain why they also purr when giving birth, frightened, or severely injured. Experts have identified three different purr types:

1. The purr that signals contentment

2. The solicitation purr (a more urgent and less calming purr that cats use when they want something)

3. The healing purr

Evidence for the benefits of purring is mounting. The findings of various studies indicate that the vibrational frequency of a cat's purr may provide healing and perhaps even health protection benefits, not only for cats but for humans as well.

Researchers have found that consistent vibrational sound frequencies of 25-150 Hz, which is the range of a cat's purr, speed the healing of bones, tendons, ligaments, and muscles as well as providing pain relief (Von Muggenthaler, 2001).

Purring increases bone strength, speeds healing

Cats' bones heal faster and more easily after fractures than those of dogs, which is why 90% of cats that plummet from extraordinary heights survive despite serious injuries (Whitney & Mehlhaff, 1987). There is also evidence that cats are less likely to suffer postoperative complications after surgery than dogs, and this rapid healing ability may be attributable to purring (Von Muggenthaler, 2001).

Cats also suffer from bone diseases far less often than dogs, and it's likely that purring plays a role in this. There are a number of osteo diseases that are rare in cats but common in dogs, including scapulohumeral joint luxations and hip dysplasia. Cats are also less likely to suffer from osteosarcoma, osteoarthritis, and myeloma (a tumour of the bone marrow's plasma cells) (Von Muggenthaler, 2001).

Researcher Clinton Rubin and his colleagues have discovered that sound frequencies of 20-50 Hz can increase bone density, and when they placed chickens on a vibrating plate for 20 minutes each day, they found that the chickens grew stronger bones (Von Muggenthaler, 2001). This finding was replicated in a study of rabbits, during which bone strength increased by 20% after exposure to the 20-50Hz sound frequency, and the healing of broken bones and the speed of bone regeneration were accelerated (Chen, Han, & Yang, 1994).

The effect of the purr frequency on bones has significant implications, given the large number of people who suffer from osteoporosis (bone loss) as they age. Dr. Rubin and his colleagues have continued to conduct research in this field that may yield treatments for osteoporosis and other bone-related problems in humans (Rubin et al., 2001; Rubin et al., 2004; Rubin, Judex, & Qin, 2006).

Additional benefits of purring

Lungs: Research indicates that purring can help decrease dyspnea, or shortness of breath, a symptom of chronic obstructive pulmonary disease. One study found that among dogs and cats suffering from myocardial necrosis, all of the dogs had dyspnea, but none of the cats suffered from this condition (Kidd, Stepien, & Amrheiw, 2000). Researchers have also found that in humans, a vibration of 100 Hz (which is in the purr range) can decrease dyspnea (Cristiano & Schwartzstein, 1997; Nakayama et al., 1998; Sibuya et al., 1994). Moreover, the incidence of primary lung tumours is three times higher in dogs than in cats (Miles, 1988).

Muscles and ligaments: Cats suffer from diseases afflicting the muscles and ligaments far less often than dogs, and low-decibel frequencies similar to those of a cat's purr can speed the healing of muscles and tendons in humans (Von Muggenthaler, 2001). One study found that after sustaining sports injuries, low-frequency biomechanical stimulation prevented decreases in muscle strength and mass (Lake, 1992). Another study found that the purr-frequency vibration can speed tendon healing in the ankle, increasing upper ankle joint mobility by up to 19% after injury (Klysczt et al., 1997).

Pain: Research has shown that exposure to a sound frequency between 50 and 150 Hz provides relief for 82% of those suffering chronic and acute pain (Lundeberg, 1983). Given the pain-relief benefits of the purr vibration, it's unsurprising that cats often purr when they are injured or giving birth.

Resident cat Sage washes a young orphaned foster kitten named Gizmo, Jennifer Copley

Sage hugs another foster kitten named Alta, Jennifer Copley

Tesla purring, Jennifer Copley

References

- Chen, L.P.; Han, Z.B.; & Yang, X.Z. (1994). "The Effects of Frequency of Mechanical Vibration on Experimental Fracture Healing." *Zhonghua Wai Ke Za Zhi (Chinese Journal of Surgery)*, 32(4), pp. 217-219.
- Cristiano, L.M., & Schwartzstein, R.M. (1997). "Effect of Chest Wall Vibration on Dyspnea During Hypercapnia and Exercise in Chronic Obstructive Pulmonary Disease." *American Journal of Respitory Critical Care Medicine*, 155(5), pp. 1552-1559.
- Kidd, L.; Stepien, R.L.; & Amrheiw, D.P. (2000). "Clinical Findings and Coronary Artery Disease in Dogs and Cats with Acute and Subacute Myocardial Necrosis: 28 Cases." *Journal of the American Animal Hospital Association*, 36(3), pp. 199-208.
- Klyscz, T.; Ritter-Schempp, C.; Junger, M.; & Rassner, G. (1997). "Biomechanical Stimulation Therapy as Physical Treatment of Arthrogenic Venous Insufficiency." *Hautarzt*, 48(5), pp. 318-322.
- Lake, D.A. (1992). "Neuromuscular Electrical Stimulation. An Overview and Its Application in the Treatment of Sports Injuries." *Sports Medicine*, 13(5), pp. 320-336.
- Lundeberg, T.C. (1983). "Vibratory Stimulation for the Alleviation of Chronic Pain." *ACTA Physiologica Scandinavica*, 523(Suppl.), 1-51.
- Lyons, L. (3 April 2006). "Why Do Cats Purr." *Scientific American*, ScientificAmerican.com.
- Miles, K.G. (1988). "A Review of Primary Lung Tumors in the Dog and Cat." *Veterinary Radiology*, 29(3), pp. 122–128.
- Nakayama, H.; Shibuya, M.; Yamada, M.; Suzuki, H.; Arakawa, M.; & Homma, I. (1998). "In-Phase Chest Wall Vibration Decreases Dyspnea During Arm Elevation in Chronic Obstructive Pulmonary Disease Patients." *Internal Medicine*, 37(10), pp. 831-835.
- Rubin, C.T.; Judex, S.; & Qin, Y.X. (2006). "Low-Level Mechanical Signals and Their Potential as a Non-Pharmacologic Intervention for Osteoporosis." *Age and Ageing*, 35(Suppl.), pp. 32-36.
- Rubin, C.T.; Recker, R.; Cullen, D.; Ryaby, J.; McCabe, J.; & McLeod, K.J. (2004) "Prevention of Post-Menopausal Bone Loss by a Low Magnitude, High Frequency Mechanical Stimuli: A Clinical Trial Assessing Compliance, Efficacy and Safety." *Journal of Bone & Mineral Research*, 19(3), pp. 343-351.

- Rubin, C.T.; Turner, A.S.; Bain, S.; & Mallinckrodt, M. (2001). "Anabolism. Low Mechanical Signals Strengthen Long Bones." *Nature*, 412(6847), pp. 603-604.
- Sibuya, M.; Yamada, M.; Kanamaru, A.; Tanaka, K.; Suzuki, H.; Noguchi, E.; Altose, M.D.; & Homma, I. (1994). "Effect of Chest Wall Vibration on Dyspnea with Chronic Respiratory Disease." *American Journal of Respitory and Critical Care Medicine*, 149(5), pp. 1235-1240.
- Stuart, A. (Reviewed by Cook, A., BVM&S). (2012). "Why Cats Purr." *Healthy Cats.* WebMD.com.
- Von Muggenthaler E., Fauna Communications Research Institute. (2001). "The Felid Purr: A Bio-Mechanical Healing Mechanism." Presented and published in the proceedings from the 12th International Conference on Low Frequency Noise and Vibration and its Control held in Bristol, UK, 18th to 20th September, 2006. Also Presented at the 2001, 142nd annual Acoustical Society of America, American Institute of Physics, International Conference.
- Whitney, W.O, & Mehlhaff, C.J. (1987). "High-Rise Syndrome in Cats." *Journal of the American Veterinary Medical Association*, 191(11), pp. 1399-1403.

Chapter 13: Other Frequently Asked Questions

A cat relaxes on a sun-warmed concrete perch, Jennifer Copley

Do cats like music?

A foster kitten on a drum, Jennifer Copley

Feline reactions to music are quite variable, ranging from fear and loathing to indifference to love of certain musical genres. There hasn't been much research conducted to examine feline musical preferences, but there have been several interesting studies, as well as many amusing anecdotal reports.

Music cats like

Austrian scientists have found that cats appear to prefer instruments such as the oboe and deep bass, as well as male voice choirs. They made this discovery by filming cats as they listened to various types of music and observing whether they moved closer to or further away from the speakers. Overall, they found that cats prefer fast beats to slow beats, and deep tones to high-pitched notes.

Many people claim that their cats prefer the genre of music they themselves prefer, whereas others have experienced conflicts. One owner who regularly left her radio set to an easy listening station claimed that her Siamese cat changed it to hard rock every time she went out (how he did this was not specified).

Some cats have shown an interest in playing musical instruments, particularly the piano. Search YouTube and you'll find plenty of feline musicians, many of which have selected the piano as their instrument of choice.

Composer Henri Sauguet's cat Cody reacted with what appeared to be ecstatic joy when he played Debussy on the piano, racing over to lick Sauguet's hands. However, zoologist Desmond Morris speculates that rather than enjoying the music, Cody found certain notes similar to the sounds of a kitten in distress and was trying to comfort his owner. This explains why cats often run to and interfere with people who are playing certain musical notes, but not why some cats seem to enjoy banging away on the piano themselves.

Writer Theophile Gautier found that although his cat would listen attentively when he played the piano, she would become upset whenever the accompanying singer struck a high note, reaching out to cover the woman's mouth with her paw. Drs. Bachrach and Morin replicated this finding in the 1930s, discovering that high notes caused many cats to become agitated, while a fourth-octave E note induced sexual excitement in adult cats. These findings support the theory that some feline reactions to music occur because certain notes mimic natural feline language.

Feline music critics

Many cats find loud music upsetting, but this is true of other animals as well. A study in which mice were subjected to heavy metal music blasted around the clock to gauge music's effects on learning had to be cut short when the mice all killed each other. Some cats are also averse to high-pitched instruments even when the music is not played loudly. In one extreme case a cat actually suffered convulsions in response to certain notes.

A few cats have had particularly extreme musical aversions. The Mini-Annals of Improbable Research (a free newsletter featuring strange research studies, inventions, and discoveries) summarizes a case study of a cat that reacted hysterically to the theme music for Star Trek and showed signs of paranoia for some time even after the music had stopped.

Mood music for cats

Animal behaviourist Hermann Bubna-Littitz, after studying music's effects on cats, created a song compilation called "Music for Cats and Friends" designed to calm anxious cats. The CD contains electronically synthesized variants of a number of popular tunes such as "Memories," "Moonlight Walk," and "Endless Time."

There is also a CD available called "Relaxation Music for Dogs and Cats," a synthesized environmental soundscape targeted toward the broader sound range perceptible to cats and dogs. A third offering is "Music for Cats...and People Too!" This species-defying compilation encompasses jazz, classical, natural-environmental, and ambient styles and makes use of a wide range of instruments.

In 2015, Snowdon et al. created a compilation of music specifically designed for cats to support their research on species-appropriate music, which includes songs pitched to a frequency based on cat vocalizations rather than human speech and drum tempos that evoke feline purring and suckling. Cats reacted to this music by becoming excited, approaching the source of the sound, and rubbing their bodies against the speakers, whereas they showed no interest in classical music.

More research is required

With the exception of responses to high notes, feline reactions to music are quite variable and idiosyncratic. There hasn't been enough research conducted to draw definitive conclusions as to whether cats enjoy some types of music or simply react instinctively to certain notes and beats. Hopefully someone within the scientific community will pursue this amusing area of inquiry in the future.

References

- "Cat Behaviour (2)." (7 November 1998). Mini-Annals of Improbable Research (Mini-Air). BUBL.ac.uk.
- CatsandKittens.com. (2008). "Cats: Does Music Mellow Them?"
- CatsInternational.org. (2007). "Musical Cats."
- Chapman, C. (n.d.). "Cool Cats Have Natural Rhythm." *Sunday Times*. PetsandMusic.com.
- McDonald, F. (2018). "Scientists Have Created the Perfect Music for Cats." ScienceAlert.com.
- Morris, D. (1987). *Catlore*. London, UK: Jonathan Cape Ltd.
- Snowdon, C.T., Teie, D., & Savage, M. (2015). "Cats prefer species-appropriate music." *Applied Animal Behaviour Science, 166*, 106-111.
- Wertz, M. (7 February 1998). "Why Classical Music Is the Key to Education" in *The Schiller Institute's Towards a New Renaissance in Classical Education*, Schillerinstitute.org.

Does spaying or neutering affect a cat's behaviour and personality?

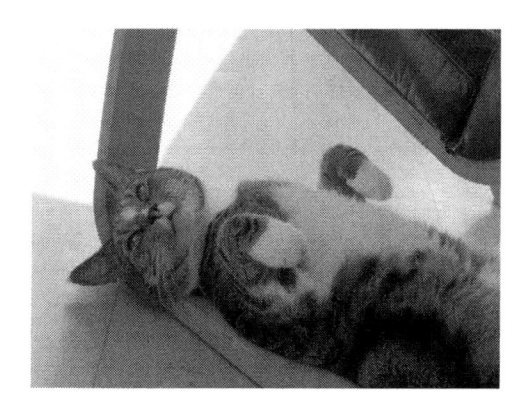

A neutered adult male cat, Jennifer Copley

Most cat owners realize that having pets sterilized is the right thing to do, but many have concerns about the potential effects of these surgeries on the personalities of their companion animals. The following are summaries of expert opinions regarding behavioural and personality changes as a result of spay-neuter surgeries.

Behavior changes

According to the University of California School of Veterinary Medicine, spaying or neutering a cat will reduce or eliminate a number of undesirable hormone-related behaviours, including urine spraying and fighting in males, and problems associated with heat cycles in females, such as irritability, yowling to attract mates, and drawing aggressive, noisy males to the area.

Pets that have been spayed or neutered are less inclined to escape from the house and roam, which significantly reduces the likelihood that they will get lost or be run over by cars; injured in fights with other animals; infected with viruses, bacteria, or parasites; or stolen by pet thieves.

Overall, sterilization surgery reduces the majority of problem behaviours in companion animals, so spayed and neutered animals are far less likely to be surrendered to shelters for severe behavioural issues than unaltered pets.

Personality effects

According to the University of California School of Veterinary Medicine, spay-neuter surgeries don't typically change aspects of personality such as playfulness, vocalization, hunting skills, or desire for activity. However, evidence suggests that some fixed pets become more docile or laid back because hormone-related anxiety and aggression are reduced or eliminated, and many pets become more affectionate after the surgery.

Some pet owners are concerned that male cats will feel less masculine or suffer some sort of identity crisis as a result of neutering surgery. This worry arises from the tendency to project human feelings onto animals. Animals don't have a sexual identity that affects their psychological state or a culture in which gender is relevant, so they don't experience gender identity trauma as a result of sterilization.

Benefits

Spaying and neutering can provide a number of benefits, including:

- Reduced risk of breast cancer in females (this disease is fatal for about 90% of cats, according to the ASPCA)
- Prevention of uterine and ovarian cancer, as well as severe uterine infections such as pyometra (a common problem that requires hospitalization, antibiotics, intravenous fluids, and emergency spaying)
- Prevention of testicular cancer and reduced risk for prostate cancer in males
- Significantly reduced risk of developing genito-urinary problems
- Decreased anxiety, aggression, and fighting, which reduces the risk of fight-related injuries and abscesses
- Reduced compulsion to escape and roam, which lowers the risk of pet theft, infectious diseases such as rabies and Feline Immunodeficiency Virus (FIV), and car accidents
- Reduction or elimination of undesirable behaviours such as urine marking in both genders
- Reduced shedding in females

Some people believe that females should be allowed to have a litter before spaying. However, female cats enjoy better health and longevity if they are spayed without having any litters, and early spaying has no negative psychological effects.

Risks and recovery

Although all surgeries present some degree of risk, spaying and neutering are considered routine, low-risk surgeries. The risks to unfixed animals are far more significant, as they have a greater likelihood of suffering from fatal diseases and accidents. Pets that have been spayed or neutered live 30% longer, on average, because of the health and behavioural benefits provided by the surgery.

Pets can usually be dropped off at a clinic in the morning and retrieved later the same day, though in some cases an overnight stay is required. Owners are given instructions for post-surgical care, which usually include restricting activity for a week or less.

Recovery times vary based on an animal's age. Younger animals usually recover very quickly (kittens may take only a day or two). Older pets usually take a little longer. Most pets are back to normal within a few days.

Resident cat Freya snuggles with Nova, Jennifer Copley

Metabolic effects

Many pet owners are concerned that their pets will become lazy and obese after sterilization surgery because their metabolisms are a little slower. However, according to experts, obesity in animals is more likely to result from feeding too much cheap pet food. Cats become overweight and suffer health problems when fed a low-quality, high-carbohydrate diet because they are obligate carnivores (animals that meet their nutritional requirements with meat).

Pets that are sterilized at a young age tend to be longer and taller when full-grown, but not necessarily fatter. Some altered pets may have an increased risk of obesity because they don't roam far away from the house, so they get less exercise, but animals that are walked or played with regularly and fed appropriate portions of high-quality food are unlikely to become obese.

Ideal age for sterilization surgery

Many pets are capable of procreating as early as 5 months of age, so they should be spayed or neutered before adolescence. Based on recent studies, many veterinarians are endorsing very early spay-neuter surgeries, as animals neutered at a young age recover more quickly.

References

- ASPCA. (2010). "Top 10 Reasons to Spay or Neuter Your Pet." ASPCA.org.
- Cruden, D., Winn Feline Foundation. (1992). "Early Spay/Neuter in the Cat." Cat Fanciers' Association. CFA.org.
- Day, J.W., DVM. (2007). "Why Spaying and Neutering Is Important for Pet Health." FamilyVet.com.
- Plotnick, A., DVM. (2006). "Spaying and Neutering: Facts, Myths, and Misconceptions." ManhattanCats.com.
- Sacramento SPCA. (2008). "Why You Should Spay or Neuter Your Pet." SSPCA.org.
- Second Time Around Aussie Rescue. (n.d.). "Frequently Asked Questions About Spaying and Neutering." STAAR.org.
- Tierney, R., Partnership for Animal Welfare. (n.d.). "Spaying and Neutering." Paw-Rescue.org.
- University of California School of Veterinary Medicine. (n.d.). "Spaying or Neutering Your Cat." VMTH.UCDavis.edu.

Can indoor cats be happy?

Resident cat Freya hugs foster kitten Leo, Jennifer Copley

In recent years, various experts have concluded that cats can be happy with an indoor lifestyle if the environment provides everything a cat needs to fulfill his wild urges.

Animal behaviour specialists have only recently begun to study cat psychology. In the past, little was known about the psychological needs of cats, and this lack of knowledge has contributed to the following misconceptions.

Myth 1: A cat can't follow his true nature unless he's free to roam.

Cats spend most of their time sleeping, grooming, hunting, scratching, and observing the world. A cat sleeping indoors enjoys his snooze just as much as an outdoor cat, but he's far less likely to pick up fleas and ticks or be attacked by another animal while he sleeps, and a cat with access to window perches or a screened balcony or porch can enjoy fresh air, sunshine, and outdoor scenery without the risk being attacked or run over by a car.

Cats do need to hunt, but this can happen indoors if you provide plenty of toys and engage in interactive play activities that simulate the hunt. Cats with opportunities to mock-hunt (capture a catnip mouse, a rolling ball, a feather on a wand toy, etc.) tend to be happier.

Providing cat trees or other perches, hiding places, and cat-safe plants helps to simulate the outdoor environment as well, and good scratch post is particularly important. For those who want to provide a more natural scratching experience, most cats enjoy scratching tree bark. A tree stump that's tall enough for the cat to stand upright and scratch is usually appreciated, though most cats are happy to scratch a manufactured post covered with carpet or wrapped in sisal twine.

Myth 2: A cat won't be happy unless he can kill and eat small animals.

Cats are perfectly happy to eat the food their owners provide, and when well fed, many don't actually eat the animals they capture. Because they're carnivorous, cats require a high-protein diet, but premium cat foods that have meat as their first ingredient can provide good nutrition without the risk of picking up diseases from the carcases of infected rodents and birds.

Kismet pauses for a photo while sneaking up on resident cat Laya, Jennifer Copley

Young Sage contemplates pouncing on a toy, Jennifer Copley

Myth 3: Cats are independent and asocial; they need to go off on their own.

Contrary to the image of the solitary, independent cat, feral cats live in colonies, form friendships with other cats, and collaboratively raise and protect kittens, and most domestic cats are happy to incorporate humans and other pets into their social groups. Wild cats hunt on their own because they catch prey only large enough to feed one cat – not because they want to be alone.

Sola and Raya hang out together on a cat tree, Jennifer Copley

Myth 4: Cats should be allowed to hunt outdoors because they fill a critical ecological niche as predators.

Domestic cats are the descendants of African wild cats. Early domesticated cats were brought along on cargo ships to catch rodents that would otherwise eat the travelers' food stores and then deposited at ports in various countries. Cats are not a natural element in most ecosystems where they now reside, and they can deplete the supply of prey needed by native predators such as owls and hawks and decimate local bird populations when allowed to roam freely.

Myth 5: Indoor cats are missing out on something vital.

Many people argue that it's natural for a cat to go outside – after all, that's how wild cats live. But the majority of wild cats suffer frequently from hunger, parasite infestations, diseases, and other natural dangers. Domestic cats with outdoor access have far shorter lives, on average, than indoor cats – the average lifespan of an indoor cat is 10 years longer than that of a free-roaming cat.

Outdoor cats are far more likely to suffer injuries as a result of car accidents or attacks by other animals. They are also more likely to ingest poison, contract communicable diseases, and transmit diseases to humans. Some outdoor cats beat the odds and live for a long time without incident, but many are killed by cars or other hazards while still very young.

Myth 6: Letting cats outdoors saves time and money because you don't have to maintain a litter box.

Owners who let their cats out may avoid litter box duties and kitty litter costs, but they're far more likely to incur large veterinary expenses due to the many hazards facing outdoor cats. In addition to injuries, ticks, and diseases, owners of outdoor cats may have to wash substances or cut burrs out of fur, remove porcupine quills, deal with skunk spray, and have their homes infested with fleas.

Outdoor cats may also anger neighbours if they use gardens or children's sandboxes as litter boxes or attack birds at neighbours' birdfeeders, creating hostile situations that cause stress for their owners.

Creating an enriched environment for indoor cats

A cat-friendly home makes provisions for the fact that a cat is a different species with its own unique needs. Indoor cats may grow bored and restless (and even put on an unhealthy amount of weight) because they lack opportunities to hunt, explore, and engage in other natural behaviours. Bored or frustrated cats may tear around the house, sleep too much, overeat, behave badly, or develop pathological grooming behaviours. These problems can usually be prevented by providing an enriched home environment.

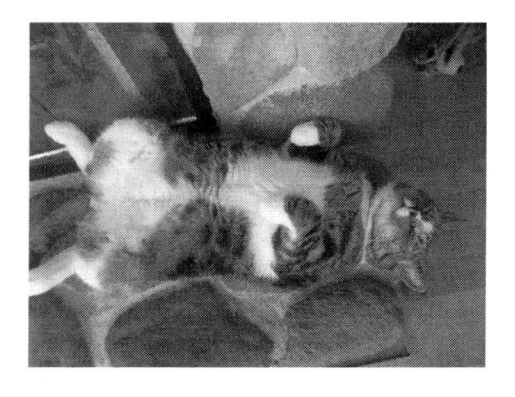

Sage relaxes by the fireplace, Jennifer Copley

Exercise and entertainment

To reduce the risk of obesity and behavioural problems resulting from boredom and lack of exercise:

- Regularly engage in interactive play that simulates the hunt. Cat Dancers and other wand toys are good for this purpose.
- Provide solo toys and rotate them regularly, hiding some and bringing others out so that the cat doesn't grow bored with them. Toy mice are usually a hit, and items lying around the house such as cardboard boxes and paper bags make good toys as well.
- Buy or build a cat tree to provide climbing opportunities and a high perch.
- Build or purchase a sturdy scratch post that is tall enough or long enough for the cat to stretch out while scratching.
- Screen in a window so it can be opened to provide fresh air. For a stylish viewing space, a feline perch, window veranda, or solarium can be added.
- Provide a little catnip from time to time so that cats can enjoy a fun, healthy high.

Resident cat Smokey and foster kitten Leo watch an interesting bug, Jennifer Copley

Resident cat Freya hangs out with foster kitten Sola, Jennifer Copley

Brasti and Dari practice their fighting skills, Jennifer Copley

Natural feeding approaches

Cats can be fed and watered in ways that support more natural eating and drinking behaviours:

- Hide high-protein dry food or healthy treats around the house to provide foraging opportunities and the joy of discovery a cat would have in the wild.
- Place food and water bowls in separate locations. Wild cats seek food at water in different places at different times. Finding water away from a food source encourages cats to drink more, which reduces the risk of health problems, particularly for cats consuming an all-dry diet.

- Invest in a pet water fountain. Many cats prefer drinking from a fountain to still water because it resembles natural running water.
- Grow cat grass (oat grass) indoors to provide some natural vegetation.

Psychological needs

In addition to love, affection, and companionship, feline psychological requirements include privacy and control of resources. To keep cats happy and avoid conflicts:

- Provide at least one private space for each cat in a multi-cat household. This could be a fancy kitty condo or just a cardboard box with a hole in it. Don't disturb cats when they retreat to their private spaces unless absolutely necessary.
- Give each cat his own food and water bowls, toys, litter box, and other resources. This reduces the likelihood of fights, as well as the accidents that occur when one cat views a single litter box as another cat's territory and avoids it.
- Place litter boxes in quiet, low-traffic areas of the house so that cats feel safe using them. Avoid perfumed litters, as the smells are unnatural, and some cats will refuse to use them.
- Although more independent than dogs, cats should not be left alone for long stretches of time. Those who spend a lot of time away from home should consider getting two compatible cats rather than adopting just one or having a friend or family member spend time with the cat when they are absent.

References

- Christensen, W. (2002). *The Humane Society of the United States Complete Guide to Cat Care*. New York, NY: St. Martin's Press.
- Halls, V., Feline Advisory Bureau. "The Cat-Friendly Home." FabCats.org.
- Ohio State University College of Veterinary Medicine. (2009). "Indoor Cat Initiative." Vet.Ohio-State.edu.

Sage hangs out with a litter of foster kittens, Jennifer Copley

Freya, Sage, and foster kitten Helix play together on a cat tree, Jennifer Copley

Do cats have psychic intuition?

Kest reacting to something humans can't hear, Jennifer Copley

There are many anecdotal accounts of cats displaying what appear to be supernatural abilities. These typically fall into three categories – prediction, navigation, and intuition.

Prediction

Many cats know when their owners will soon be arriving home, even if it's not the usual time. A cat will often become excited or run to the door shortly before her human companion's arrival (or hide under the bed well in advance of a stranger's approach). Cats have also been known to hide or rush out of buildings, bringing their kittens with them, prior to earthquakes. Such behaviors have led many people to believe that cats have predictive abilities. However, most (if not all) of these behaviors are attributable to the cat's superior sensory abilities.

Cats can hear sounds and detect smells and vibrations that people cannot. In a sense, this does give them predictive abilities. They can hear an owner's distinctive footfalls from a distance, before he turns the key in the lock, and perhaps even recognize the sounds made by his particular mode of transportation whether it is a car, a bicycle, or even a skateboard.

As for earthquakes, there have been several theories proposed. One is that animals feel subtle vibrations that precede an earthquake. Another is that they are sensitive to charged ions released into the atmosphere shortly before an earthquake occurs.

Navigation

There are many stories of cats that have traveled great distances to be reunited with their owners, leading some to believe that they use psychic powers to find the people they love. However, when a magnet is attached to a cat, his navigation skills are disrupted, which indicates that cats make use of the earth's magnetic field for wayfinding. Thus, the ability of a cat to return home over large distances is probably attributable to his finely tuned perceptive abilities rather than some sort of supernatural power.

Intuition

Often, when all seems calm, a cat will suddenly become alarmed, staring intently at something that humans cannot perceive, perhaps even growling and hissing. These behaviours have caused many to believe that cats can tune in to the spirit world. However, a cat that appears to be reacting to nothing is likely picking up on some sound or smell emanating from the material world that is too subtle or far away for humans to register.

Many cats do appear to have intuitive powers. For example, they often know when the people they care about are unhappy or not feeling well, even if those people do not show it overtly, or at least not in any way that other humans would recognize. Cats have also detected cancerous growths and predicted seizures in humans.

As impressive as these feats are, the most likely explanation is that metabolic changes accompanying illness or small physical precursors to seizures are perceptible to cats due to their finely tuned senses. Sensitive cats may also pick up on subtle aspects of body language in their human companions that indicate sickness or sadness.

Psychic pets

There are a number of reputable believers in feline psychic ability. Those who assert that cats and other animals possess supernatural intuition include Cambridge University's world-renowned biologist, Dr. Rupert Sheldrake, who has studied more than 1,000 reports of psychic connections between people and animals.

Sheldrake has noted that some cats and dogs respond to the death or suffering of their owners even when far away from them, predict dangerous events such as bombings, know when a loved one is calling on the phone before the call has been answered, and hide in anticipation of a visit to the veterinarian well before their owners haul out the pet carrier. A few other researchers also believe that cats are clairvoyant and telepathic, including Dr. J. B. Rhine.

Hailed as the father of modern-day parapsychology, J. B. Rhine (now deceased) studied Psi Trailing in animals, a phenomenon whereby animals travel long distances to find their owners. Although animals navigate using the earth's magnetic field, this doesn't explain cases of lost pets that returned to their human families after they had moved far away to places the animals had never been.

Skeptics, such as renowned zoologist and ethologist Desmond Morris, claim that in such cases, a stray animal that looks like the original pet happens to show up at the family home and wishful thinking causes the owners to assume that the hopeful stray is actually a long-lost pet. However, some of the animals that turned up on their families' doorsteps had unique features that were used to positively identify them.

Sugar, a cat who found his family 1,500 miles away in their new home, was recognized due to his unusual bone deformity. In preparation for an impending move, the family had regretfully given Sugar to their neighbours as they thought the long car journey would be too hard on him, but traveling on foot by himself, the cat somehow managed to find them. Sugar walked from California to Oklahoma, an incredible journey that took more than a year, to be reunited with the family he loved.

A similar authenticated case is that of a veterinarian who moved from New York to California, leaving his cat in the care of others back in New York. Several months later, a cat that looked much like his came strolling into his new residence. Not inclined to make assumptions, the vet thoroughly inspected the new arrival. To his amazement, he found a telltale bone growth on the cat's fourth tail vertebra, the result of a long-ago bite that his cat had sustained. Thus, he determined that his cat had indeed traveled over 2,500 miles of unfamiliar terrain to find him.

The debate continues

Of course, it is possible that the widespread phenomena noted by Sheldrake, Rhine, and other researchers have scientific explanations that have not yet been discovered. In the meantime, the skeptics will remain skeptical, arguing that much of the evidence for feline extrasensory perception is anecdotal and probably the result of coincidence, while believers in feline psychic abilities will continue to believe, asserting that such phenomena are too common and universal to be dismissed.

References

- BBC News. (13 June 2006). "Hero Cat Predicts Epileptic Fits." News.bbc.co.uk.
- Brown, D.J. (n.d.). "Etho-Geological Forecasting: Unusual Animal Behavior and Earthquake Prediction." *Mavericks of the Mind: Conversations for the New Millennium*. Users.Lycaeum.org/~Maverick.
- Canfield, J.; Hansen, M.V.; Becker, M.; & Kline, C. (1999). *Chicken Soup for the Cat and Dog Lover's Soul*. Deerfield Beach, Florida: Health Communications Inc.
- Cooper, P.; Noble, P.I; & Fleming, J. (1997). *277 Secrets Your Cat Wants You To Know: A Cat-Alog Of Unusual and Useful Information*. Berkeley, CA: Ten Speed Press.
- Morris, D. (1987). *Catlore*. London: Jonathan Cape Ltd.

- Mott, M. (11 November 2003). "Can Animals Sense Earthquakes?" *National Geographic News*.
- Rickard, B., & Michell, J. (2000). *Unexplained Phenomena*. New York: Rough Guides.
- Schneck, M., & Caravan, J. (1990). *Cat Facts*. New York: Barnes & Noble Inc.
- Schneider, K. (16 February 2009). "Cat Nips Owner's Lung Cancer: Man Credits Feline Friend's Paws of Life for Discovery of Large Tumour." *The Calgary Sun*. CNews.canoe.ca.
- Sheldrake, R. (2000). *Dogs That Know When Their Owners Are Coming Home, And Other Unexplained Powers of Animals*. Crown Publishing Group.

Are there links between fur colour and personality?

Rambler before his point markings developed, Jennifer Copley

Because both fur colour and temperament are heritable traits, it is possible for them to be linked. Anecdotal evidence provided by veterinarians, cattery workers, and cat owners, along with a handful of studies, offer some evidence for associations between fur colour and temperament. However, these are tendencies only; there are plenty of exceptions to these rules.

White

In the past, many people assumed that white cats were either timid or not very bright, but this was a misinterpretation of their behaviour because white cats with blue eyes are often deaf. When these cats did not learn their own names, come when called, or respond appropriately to loud noises, owners mistakenly assumed that they were unintelligent or shy.

Up to 80% of white cats with blue eyes are deaf due to a genetic defect that causes the cochlea (an inner ear organ) to atrophy shortly after they are born. By contrast, only 10-20% of white cats with other eye colours are deaf, and deafness is even rarer among non-white cats and white cats with point markings such as the Siamese. Many white cats are born "odd-eyed," with one blue eye and one eye of another colour. In such cases, the cat is often deaf on the blue-eyed side but able to hear on the side with the eye of a different colour.

There is a common misconception that white cats with blue eyes are bad mothers because many do not hear their kittens calling and thus appear to be ignoring their offspring, but most deaf cats compensate well for their disability by learning to hear through their feet via sound vibrations. Their other senses may also be enhanced, enabling them to hunt effectively despite being unable to hear the movements of their prey.

The evidence regarding white cat temperament is mixed, though some surveys have found trait associations with white fur in particular breeds. For example, white Persians are thought to be calm and peaceful while white British Shorthairs are friendly and outgoing.

Red, cream, and ginger

Max looking guilty about something, Jennifer Copley

As with white cats, the evidence for temperament associations in red and cream (ginger) cats is mixed. Some surveys have found certain red and cream breeds to be even-tempered and laid back, while others have suggested that these cats (particularly the gingers) have fiery tempers, unpredictable behaviour, and less friendly dispositions. Some support for this latter observation was provided by a study conducted by Ledger and O'Farrell (1996, cited by Hartwell), which found that cream, red, and tortie kittens struggled for longer when held by unfamiliar individuals and tried harder to escape than did kittens with other fur colours.

Cattery owner George Ware (cited by Hartwell) has found ginger-and-white cats to be lazy and laid back, describing them as "big softies." On the other hand, Pontier et al. (1995) have suggested that the gene associated with orange fur may be linked to aggressiveness in males, and according to Natoli and DeVito (2001, cited by Hartwell), this may be why orange cats are relatively rare in urban high-density feral colonies compared to the more easy-going black and black-and-white cats. Because female cats are promiscuous, in large, crowded colonies, laid-back males who are willing to wait their turn will have greater reproductive success than those who waste their time and energy fighting.

Tortoiseshell and calico

Scamper hanging out on my desk, Jennifer Copley

The coats of tortoiseshell cats are made up of mottled orange and black patches (or cream and blue-gray for dilute tortoiseshells), and additional white patches in the case of calicos. Some torties have a relatively equal distribution of coloured patches, whereas others have coats made up predominantly of one colour, with just a few areas in the opposing colour. Individual sections of colour usually blend softly without clear boundaries, and flecks of one colour are often interspersed within patches of another. The coat is actually a mix of two coat types: red (orange) tabby and black. Because both these genes are sex-linked (carried on the X chromosome), only a cat with two X chromosomes can inherit the combination. Males normally have one X and one Y chromosome, so tortoiseshell and calico cats are typically female. The few males who have this coat type due to a chromosomal abnormality (XXY males) are sterile.

Tortoiseshell and calico cat temperaments may differ by breed. Surveys have found Persian calicos to be maternal and Persian tortoiseshells to be calm and sweet-natured. British Shorthairs with tortoiseshell markings are said to be quick-witted, and mixed-breed calicos to be temperamental, naughty, and lively. Cattery owner George Ware describes tortoiseshells and calicos as gentle and friendly in most cases, and notes that they often eat too much and become overweight.

For those who have an interest in breeding torties, gingers, or black cats:

- Red female + red male = red male and female kittens
- Black female + red male = black male kittens, tortie female kittens
- Tortie female + red male = red or black male kittens, red or tortie female kittens
- Tortie female + black male = red or black male kittens, tortie or black female kittens
- Red female + black male = red male kittens, tortie female kittens
- Black female + black male = black male and female kittens

Results may vary a little because the expression of genes can either increase the tortie appearance or disguise it, so some cats that appear to be solid red or black may actually be torties. It's also difficult to breed specifically for calicos, though having one black and one red parent may increase the chances.

Colourpoint

Helix, a flame-point, Jennifer Copley

Cats with coloured point markings such as the Siamese and various Siamese crossbreeds (including the Balinese, Burmese, Colourpoint Shorthair, Himalayan, Javanese, Ocicat, Oriental Shorthair and Longhair, Snowshoe, and Tonkinese) tend to be extroverted, spirited, inquisitive, clever, talkative, and active. Most colourpoint cats have personality traits similar to those of their Siamese cousins, though these traits may be modified by the tendencies of other breeds that were used in their breed development programs.

Tabby

Sage requesting a treat, Jennifer Copley

All striped domestic cats are tabbies, and experts believe that the tabby is the wild type (original coat type) of all domestic cats. This coat type was probably selected for because it provides good camouflage for hunting and avoiding predators. In addition to the stripes on their bodies, typical tabby markings include lines around the eyes and on the cheeks and a letter "M" on the forehead. There are four tabby types:

- Classic/blotched: Swirling or marbled patterns
- Mackerel: Narrow parallel vertical stripes down the sides of the body
- Spotted: Spots (large or small) or broken parallel stripes over the sides of the body
- Ticked: Tabby markings on the face but no stripes or spots over the rest of the body where the fur has alternating bands of lighter and darker colour; found in breeds such as the Abyssinian, Somali, and Singapura as well as various non-purebreds

Tabby colour schemes include:

- Blue: Dark gray or blue-gray stripes on a lighter gray or off-white background

- Brown: Black or dark brown stripes on a brown or grayish background
- Cream: Darker cream (peach or sand-coloured) stripes over a lighter cream background
- Red: Dark orange or marmalade stripes over a cream background
- Silver: Black, gray, cream, orange, brown, lilac, or fawn stripes on a white or off-white background (those with orange stripes are known as cameo tabbies)

Surveys indicate that cats with tabby markings tend to be good-natured, affable, home-loving, and languid. Cattery owner George Ware says that tabbies are usually friendly, relaxed, and somewhat lazy.

Black

Callisto, Jennifer Copley

Traits that have been associated with black cats in various studies and by anecdotal evidence include friendliness, loyalty, stubbornness, and a generally good-natured personality.

Many assume the genetic mutation that produced black fur was selected for because it provides better camouflage. However, gene studies conducted at the US National Cancer Institute have linked black fur with a gene family involved in a number of illnesses, which suggests that black cats may be more resistant to certain diseases. This theory is supported by the fact that black and black-and-white cats are more abundant than those of other fur colours in feral colonies where virus resistance would be particularly beneficial because close proximity with other animals increases the likelihood of catching diseases.

Fur colours such as brown (ranging from dark chocolate to light cinnamon) arise from a mutation in the gene that produces black fur, so it's possible that brown cats enjoy similar health benefits.

Sadly, although black cats often have the best temperaments (and perhaps the best health prospects as well), they are the least likely to be adopted, and many are euthanized at shelters as a result.

Animal rescue organizations have noted that black cats are at a significant disadvantage when it comes to adoption. A 2002 California study found that black cats were only half as likely to find loving homes as tabbies, and two-thirds less likely to be adopted than cats with white fur. Given that overall adoption rates were just 20% for all shelter cats, black cats have particularly bleak odds.

Ignorant superstition is the primary reason why people fail to adopt black cats, and it may account for the fact that most black cats have a few white hairs. Zoologist Desmond Morris has suggested that having some white fur was advantageous during the European witch craze that spanned the fifteenth through early eighteenth centuries. During this dark era when irrationality and hysteria led to the deaths of an enormous number of innocent people and animals, black cats were particular targets for persecution. Having a few white hairs may have saved a cat from being killed, so the gene pool was divested of completely black cats over the course of many years.

In the past, black cats were often portrayed negatively in literary works and suffered from prejudice and ignorance, so many attribute their low adoption rate to this lasting stigma (this problem affects black dogs to a lesser extent as well). To make matters worse, because they have dark coats, black cats may not be as noticeable in photographs, so they are less likely to attract attention than their more colourful counterparts.

Many black cats are counted among the feline heroes who have made history and headlines, including Homer, who attacked a home invader to save his owner; Luna, who woke her owners in the night so they could escape a house fire; and Schnautzie, who alerted her owners to a gas leak, saving them from dying in an explosion. Many black cats have also been featured in stories about seeing eye cats, therapy cats, seizure-alert cats, and cats that have provided direct help or sought assistance from others for owners who suffered medical crises.

Black and white

Catisse on my desk, Jennifer Copley

Is there a bicolour personality that differs from the typical black cat temperament? Bicolour cats have rarely been studied individually, although there was one Bavarian study which found that black and white cats were more likely to wander far from home than cats of other coat types. Owner surveys also suggest that the black-and-white cat temperament is usually placid, even, and friendly.

Rush Shippen Huidekoper wrote unfavourably about black and white cats in his 1895 book, *The Cat*, noting that they tended "...more than any other cat to become fat and indolent, or ragged and wretched, as the case may be." He did go on to say that "the black-and-white cat is affectionate and cleanly," but then qualified this statement by asserting that it is "...a selfish animal, and is not one for children to play with."

Despite this unpromising historical description, there are plenty of anecdotal reports from owners and veterinarians ascribing good temperament and friendliness to black and whites. Cattery owner George Ware praises black and white cats as "true lap cats" that are "very loyal to their family," though he does note that they are "liable to be moody."

Black and white cats are overrepresented among the most famous felines of all time, including:

- Socks, a cat owned by US president Bill Clinton
- Humphrey, Chief Mouser to the Cabinet Office at 10 Downing Street (official residence of the UK Prime Minister), 1988-2006
- Lewis, a polydactyl cat that made headlines after he was placed under house arrest for attacking people
- Simon, a wartime hero who served aboard the HMS Amethyst, protecting food stores from rats
- Oscar (a.k.a. Unsinkable Sam), who survived the sinking of three different warships and eventually retired to a home for sailors

There are also many famous fictional black and white cats, including the cartoon cats Sylvester and Fritz, and Dr. Seuss's Cat in the Hat.

A popular and controversial website, Cats That Look Like Hitler, features photos of bicolour cats whose markings cause them to resemble Adolf Hitler. The majority of these cats are black and whites with facial markings that look like the infamous black moustache and hairstyle set against a white face area. The site is loved by many but hated by more than a few, and has pages featuring both fan mail and hate mail. It should be noted that the site is not meant to glorify Hitler, but rather, to mock him. Owners of "Kitlers" are invited to send in their photos to be featured on the site (www.catsthatlooklikehitler.com).

Gray

If I fits, I sits: A foster kitten hangs out in a heavy glass vase we put in front of the cupboard doors to prevent Sage from opening the cupboard and helping himself to cat treats, Jennifer Copley

Gray fur (known as blue) is a dilute variant of black. Blue-gray fur is associated with a quiet, mellow temperament. Cats with gray coats are said to be affectionate, peaceful, calm, and gentle, though if the blue has cream tones, the disposition may be livelier.

References

- Grandin, T. (2009). *Animals Make Us Human*. New York, NY: Houghton Mifflin Harcourt.
- Hartwell, S. (2007). "Is Coat Colour Linked to Temperament?" MessyBeast.com.
- Marcus, A. (21 March 2003). "Black Cats and Genomics Cross Paths." GenomeNewsNetwork.com.
- Meyer, J.R. (1994). "Black Jaguars in Belize?: A Survey of Melanism in the Jaguar, Panthera onca." Biological-Diversity.info.
- Morris, D. (1987). *Catlore*. London, UK: Jonathan Cape Ltd.
- Muhlhausen, E. (28 April 2008). "Black Cats Unlucky at Shelters." *The Seattle Times*, SeatleTimes.nwsource.com.
- Starbuck, O., & Thomas, D. (2004). "Cat Color FAQ: Cat Color Genetics." Fanciers.com.
- Turner, D.C., & Bateson, P. (Eds.). (2000). *The Domestic Cat: The Biology of Its Behaviour*. New York, NY: Cambridge University Press.

How many hours do cats sleep?

Smokey naps on a stack of DVDs by my computer, Jennifer Copley

Adult cats spend approximately 65% of their time sleeping, or nearly 16 hours per day, though it is mostly a light sleep. Only 15% of their time is spent in deep sleep. Kittens, by contrast, alternate between deep sleep and being fully awake, dividing their time equally between these two states for the first few days of life, after which they gradually evolve the adult cat sleep pattern.

Why cats (and people) need to sleep is unknown, but severe sleep deprivation can be fatal, so it's obviously important to get enough sleep. Theories that have been advanced to explain the need for sleep include:

- Energy conservation
- Tissue repair
- Flushing toxins from the brain to reduce the risk of neurodegenerative diseases (i.e., Alzheimer's)
- Recharging neurotransmitter supplies
- Learning and forming memories

There is evidence for sleep's importance to learning and memory in cats. Researchers have found that kittens exposed to visual stimulation during the critical period for visual development form far more brain connections while sleeping than kittens that are kept awake after visual stimulation. Even if they are exposed to more hours of visual stimulation, the sleep-deprived kittens don't form as many brain connections as those allowed to sleep after the first session of visual stimulation.

References

- Seidensticker, J., & Lumpkin, S. (2006). *Cats: Smithsonian Q&A: The Ultimate Question and Answer Book*. Washington, DC: Smithsonian Books.
- Stoica, T. (2019). "Why Do We Sleep?" Scientific American (Blogs), January 25, Blogs.ScientificAmerican.com.

Do cats dream?

Scamper naps in a bookshelf, Jennifer Copley

Cats enter a sleep state called rapid eye movement (REM) just like people do, and this is the sleep phase during which most dream activity occurs.

If you watch a sleeping cat, you will notice that she sometimes engages in movement sequences that appear to mimic waking activities such as running or tackling. A sleeping cat may twitch her whiskers, flick her ears, move her paws, and even make sounds.

The purpose of dreaming is not known for sure, though there are some intriguing theories and plenty of evidence that REM sleep is very important. Like people, cats deprived of REM sleep are more aggressive, and studies of REM-deprived cats have also found an increase in eating and grooming behaviours. These findings are interesting because people are also more likely to overeat if they don't get sufficient sleep, and overgrooming in cats can be a sign of anxiety, which sleep-deprived people experience as well.

References

- Schneck, M., & Caravan, J. (1990). *Cat Facts*. New York: Barnes & Noble Inc.
- Vogel, G.W. (1976). "Archives of General Psychiatry. XXXII, 1975: A Review of REM Sleep Deprivation." *Psychoanal Q.*, 45:339, pp. 749-761.

Do cats always land on their feet?

Nimbus lands on a cushion after taking a tumble off the sofa
Jennifer Copley

Cats use their excellent sense of balance to orient themselves in space and adjust their body positioning during a fall to increase the likelihood of landing right side up. Because they have highly mobile backbones and floating collar bones (not attached to the shoulder joints), they are able to bend their bodies in ways that humans cannot.

As cats fall, they twist their bodies until an upright position is established. Cats also spread their legs in a sort of flying squirrel pose, which creates a parachute effect that slows falling and spreads the point of impact over a larger area upon landing. Kittens begin to develop the righting reflex at 3-4 weeks of age, and it is fully developed at about 7 weeks.

While the righting reflex helps cats land in the best way possible, they are not always able to get into a good position during a fall, and even when they do land right side up, they are usually injured when they fall from very high places.

In 1987, veterinarians at Manhattan's Animal Medical Center conducted a study of cats that had fallen from high-rise buildings. They found that 90% of falling cats survived, though the majority suffered serious injuries. More than one-third required life-saving treatments, while just under one-third did not require treatment. Strangely enough, they found that death was less likely when cats fell from heights of 7-32 stories rather than 2-6, possibly because cats have less time to adopt the flying squirrel pose when falling shorter distances. However, in another study of high-rise syndrome, Vnuk et al. (2004) found that the worst injuries occurred with falls from 7 stories or more. These researchers also found that the majority of falling cats were less than a year old, and while most (96.5%) survived, many suffered serious injuries such as broken limbs and thoracic damage.

These studies, while interesting, included only cats that were brought into clinics for veterinary care, so it is unknown how many cats actually died on impact.

References

- Elkes, J. (9 June 2001). "The Secret of Antigravity." Forums.anandtech.com.
- PetPlace.com. (2009). "Why Cats Land on Their Feet."
- Schultz, J.L., ASPCA Companion Animal Programs Advisor. (2009). "Feline High-Rise Syndrome." ASPCA.org.
- Seidensticker, J., & Lumpkin, S. (2006). *Cats: Smithsonian Q&A: The Ultimate Question and Answer Book.* Washington, DC: Smithsonian Books.
- Vnuk, D.; Pirkic, B.; Maticic, D.; Radisic, B.; Stejskal, M.; Babic, T.; Kreszinger, M.; & Lemo. N. (2004). "Feline High-Rise Syndrome: 119 Cases (1998-2001)." *Journal of Feline Medical Surgery, 6(5)*: 305-312.
- Whitney, W.O., & Mehlhaff, C.J. (1988). "High-Rise Syndrome in Cats." *Journal of the American Veterinary Medical Association, 192(4):* 542.

Do cats use their whiskers for balance?

Zack climbs a chair, Jennifer Copley

Whiskers act as feelers; they have no effect on balance. A cat uses her whiskers to judge whether she will fit through an opening and to navigate around obstacles in the dark, locate prey animals when hunting, and kill them quickly and cleanly.

Cats usually hunt at night, and their whiskers help them identify solid objects without actually touching them. When walking, particularly in the dark, a cat will often fan her whiskers forward to gather information about the terrain and detect air currents created by moving prey animals. Researchers have found that blindfolded cats can catch mice using their whiskers for guidance.

Never cut a cat's whiskers because this is like removing an additional sense. Not only does it impair the cat's navigational abilities, but it may cause unnecessary suffering to any prey she hunts, as she will have difficulty making a quick kill.

References

- Lopez, T., DVM (n.d.). "Cat Whiskers." Gemini Farm: Rescue Rehabilitation and Adoption for Domestic Pets and Farm Animals in Need.
- Seidensticker, J., & Lumpkin, S. (2006). *Cats: Smithsonian Q&A: The Ultimate Question and Answer Book*. Washington, DC: Smithsonian Books.

The moment Rowdy realized that she had no idea how to get down and required my assistance, Jennifer Copley

Sage with Catisse, Jennifer Copley

Shy Blue hides behind a book called *Ambient Findability*, Jennifer Copley

Sage takes a break after pulling down all the Christmas decorations and making a nest for himself, Jennifer Copley

Do cat personalities differ by breed?

Oriental Shorthair (left) and Korat (right), Heikki Siltala, Catza.net

According to the Cat Fanciers' Association (CFA) and various cat breeders and owners, some personality traits are more common in certain breeds. While there is substantial variation within each breed due to differences in socialization and life experiences, the following characteristics are common to particular breeds.

Most likely to be extroverted:

- Abyssinian
- American Curl
- Balinese
- Birman
- Bombay
- British Shorthair
- Burmese
- Colourpoint Shorthair
- Egyptian Mau
- Havana Brown
- Himalayan
- Japanese Bobtail
- Javanese
- LaPerm
- Maine Coon
- Manx
- Norwegian Forest Cat
- Oriental
- Persian
- Ragdoll
- Scottish Fold
- Siamese
- Siberian
- Singapura
- Snowshoe
- Somali
- Sphynx
- Tonkinese
- Turkish Angora
- Turkish Van

Most likely to be talkative:

- Balinese
- Burmese
- Colourpoint Shorthair
- Cornish Rex
- Devon Rex
- Egyptian Mau
- Birman
- Japanese Bobtail
- Norwegian Forest Cat
- Ocicat
- Oriental
- Siamese
- Siberian
- Snowshoe
- Sphynx
- Tonkinese
- Turkish Angora
- Turkish Van

Most likely to be lap cats:

- Birman
- Bombay
- Burmese
- Chartreux
- Cornish Rex
- Devon Rex
- Havana Brown
- LaPerm
- Nebelung
- Ocicat

- Oriental
- Persian
- Ragdoll
- Russian Blue
- Scottish Fold
- Selkirk Rex
- Siamese
- Sphynx
- Siamese

Ocicat, Heikki Siltala, Catza.net, Creative Commons 3.0

Most quiet and undemanding:

- Birman
- Bombay
- Chartreux
- Havana Brown
- Himalayan
- Nebelung
- Persian
- Ragdoll

- Russian Blue
- Scottish Fold
- Selkirk Rex

Most often described as having "doglike" traits:

- American Curl
- Burmese
- Chartreux
- Cornish Rex
- Cymric
- Devon Rex
- Japanese Bobtail
- Maine Coon
- Manx
- Ocicat
- Scottish Fold
- Siberian
- Turkish Van

Most laid back:

- American Bobtail
- American Curl
- American Shorthair
- British Shorthair
- Birman
- Burmese
- Cymric
- Egyptian Mau
- Exotic Shorthair
- Himalayan
- Japanese Bobtail
- Maine Coon
- Manx
- Norwegian Forest Cat
- Ocicat
- Persian
- Ragdoll
- Scottish Fold
- Selkirk Rex
- Siberian
- Sphynx
- Tonkinese
- Turkish Van

Most active:

- Abyssinian
- American Curl
- Balinese
- Bengal
- Burmese
- Colourpoint Shorthair
- Cornish Rex
- Devon Rex
- Egyptian Mau
- Japanese Bobtail
- Javanese
- Manx Cat
- Korat
- LaPerm
- Ocicat
- Oriental
- Siamese
- Siberian
- Singapura
- Somali
- Sphynx
- Tonkinese
- Turkish Angora
- Turkish Van

Abyssinian, Heikki Siltala, Catza.net, Creative Commons 3.0

Do cats age 7 years for every human year?

Cats don't actually age 7 years for every human year, as many people believe. Instead, they age rapidly during the first year, after which the process slows significantly.

The number of cat years equal to a single human year can only be estimated, though experts have a pretty good idea of the progression based on the ways in which cats mature over their lifespan.

In *The Cat Bible*, Tracie Hotchner offers a breakdown of human and cat years for the first year of life:

Freya with her mini-me foster kitten Sitka, Jennifer Copley

- 1-month-old kitten = 6-month-old human
- 3-month-old kitten = 4-year-old human
- 6-month-old kitten = 10-year-old human
- 8-month-old kitten = 15-year-old human
- 1-year-old kitten = 18-year-old human

After the first year, Hotchner estimates age equivalents as follows:

- 2 = 24
- 4 = 35
- 6 = 42
- 8 = 50
- 10 = 60
- 12 = 70
- 14 = 80
- 16 = 8

Veterinarian Arnold Plotnick provides a similar conversion. Although he considers cats to be a little older at 6 months and 1 year (which is probably more accurate, given that many cats can become pregnant or sire kittens as early as 5 or 6 months of age), he believes that the aging process slows to approximately 4 years for every human year after that:

- 0.5 = 15
- 1 = 24
- 2 = 28
- 3 = 32
- 4 = 36
- 5 = 40
- 6 = 44
- 7 = 48
- 8 = 52
- 9 = 56
- 10 = 60
- 11 = 64
- 12 = 68
- 13 = 72
- 14 = 76
- 15 = 80
- 16 = 84
- 17 = 88
- 18 = 92
- 19 = 96
- 20 = 100

About the Author

Jennifer Copley and her partner have fostered more than 100 kittens for a local animal charity as well as caring for many adult cats over the years. Her articles on cat care, psychology, and behavior have appeared in various online and print publications and her short fiction has been published in several print collections, including *The Body Book* and *The Art of Breaking Up*. In addition to animal rescue, her hobbies include rock climbing, trail racing, writing science fiction stories, and playing the drums.

Printed in Great Britain
by Amazon